A
PRIMER
ON
RATIONAL-
EMOTIVE
THERAPY

Windy Dryden

Raymond DiGiuseppe

Research Press
2612 North Mattis Avenue
Champaign, Illinois 61822

10 9 8 7 6 5   99 00 01 02 03 04

Cover design by Jack Davis
Composition by BookMasters
Printed by BookCrafters

ISBN 0–87822–319–3
Library of Congress Catalog Number 89–69838

CONTENTS

Introduction   1

Part I: Theory   3

Rationality versus Irrationality   3

The ABC Framework   4

Three Basic Musts   8

Interaction of A, B, and C   8

Two Basic Biological Tendencies   9

Theory of Change in RET   10

Overview of RET Theory   10

Part II: Practice   11

Step 1: Ask for a Problem   13

Client choice versus client's most
serious problem   13

When your client does not identify a
target problem   13

Step 2: Define and Agree upon the
Target Problem   15

Distinguish between an emotional and a
practical problem   15

Target inappropriate but not appropriate
negative emotions   16

Operationalize vague problems   16

Focus on helping your client change C, not A 16

When you still have not identified a problem   17

Be specific in assessing the target problem   17

Step 3: Assess C   19

Check again for an inappropriate
negative emotion   19

Focus on an emotional C 19

Clarify C 20

Understand that frustration is an A, not a C 20

Consider your client's motivation to change C 20

Avoid pitfalls in assessing C 21

Step 4: Assess A   23

Be specific in assessing A 23

Identify the part of A that triggers B 23

Remember that A can refer to many things   25

Assume temporarily that A is true   25

Avoid pitfalls in assessing A 26

When you still have not identified A 26

Agree on goals   27

Step 5: *Identify and Assess Any Secondary Emotional Problems*   31

Know when to work on the secondary emotional problem first   31

Check for an emotional problem about an appropriate negative emotion   32

Assess the presence of shame   32

Step 6: *Teach the* **B-C** *Connection*   33

Step 7: *Assess Beliefs*   35

Assess both premise and derivative forms   35

Remember the three basic musts   35

Distinguish between absolute shoulds and other shoulds   35

Use questions in assessing irrational beliefs   36

Step 8: *Connect Irrational Beliefs and* **C**   39

Step 9: *Dispute Irrational Beliefs*   41

Work to achieve the goals of disputing   41

Use questions during disputing   42

Be persistent in disputing premise or derivatives   43

Use a variety of disputing strategies   44

Use a variety of disputing styles   45

Be creative   47

Step 10: *Prepare Your Client to Deepen Conviction in Rational Beliefs*   49

Point out why weak conviction will not promote change   49

Deal with the "head-gut" issue   50

Step 11: Encourage Your Client to Put New Learning into Practice   51

Ensure that homework assignments are relevant   52

Collaborate with your client   52

Be prepared to compromise   52

Assess and troubleshoot obstacles   53

Use homework at different times during therapy   53

Step 12: Check Homework Assignments   55

Verify that your client faced *A*   55

Verify that your client changed *B*   56

Deal with failure to complete homework   56

Step 13: Facilitate the Working-through Process   57

Suggest different homework assignments for the same irrational belief   57

Discuss the nonlinear model of change   57

Encourage your client to take responsibility for continued progress   58

Part III: Case Example   59

Epilogue   77

Appendix: Special Features of Rational-Emotive Therapy—by Albert Ellis   79

References and Recommended Reading   95

About the Authors   99

INTRODUCTION

For well over a decade, we have trained numerous mental health practitioners in the basics of rational-emotive therapy (RET). During that time, we have seen the publication of many comprehensive book-length texts on RET, including some of our own (e.g., Dryden, 1987; Ellis & Dryden, 1987; Walen, DiGiuseppe, & Wessler, 1980). Indeed, we have used and recommended these texts in our basic RET training programs. However, we have often found these texts too lengthy for use in a basic instructional course on RET and wished that a "primer" for therapists were available that could provide a concise but systematic guide to the basics of RET practice. In 1988, we met in New York and decided to plan such a primer. This guide is the result.

In Part I, we briefly outline the principles we consider central to an understanding of the practical steps involved in RET. These practical steps, outlined in Part II, are presented in the order in which we recommend you apply them in clinical work with clients and in your practice in counseling one another.* Part III illustrates the application of the RET process to a specific case. Finally, an appendix by Albert Ellis provides a discussion of the special features of RET that help set it apart from other psychotherapies, especially other cognitive-behavioral approaches.

In the complex world of clinical practice, clients rarely seek help for only one emotional problem. Rather, they more often come to treatment with several seemingly separate but interlocking problems. The brief overview of RET practice presented in this primer is designed to complement rather than to replace the comprehensive texts that can help you deal with such situations and conduct RET at a more advanced level. We advise that you first read and digest the material in this primer, then consult the resources recommended at the end of this book for more detailed discussion of the therapeutic process. Many other useful materials on RET can be ordered from the Institute for Rational-Emotive Therapy, 45 East 65th Street, New York, NY 10021–6593. Telephone: (212) 535–0822.

We hope that you will consider this primer to be a helpful introduction to RET and that you will find RET to be a valuable approach in helping your clients overcome their emotional and behavioral difficulties.

---

*Peer counseling is used in all the basic training programs of the Institute for Rational-Emotive Therapy and is an excellent way of practicing RET. We strongly recommend that you consult the step-by-step guidelines in this primer regularly during peer counseling.

Part I

THEORY

In the first part of this primer, we outline some central principles of RET, first considering the meaning of the terms *rationality* and *irrationality* as they are used in RET. Next, we discuss RET's well-known *ABC* framework and define three basic *musts* that interfere with rational thinking and behavior. We subsequently describe two basic biological human tendencies that are relevant to the theory and practice of RET and briefly outline the RET theory of change. Finally, we provide a succinct overview of RET theory.

RATIONALITY VERSUS IRRATIONALITY

In RET, to be rational, one must be (a) pragmatic, (b) logical, and (c) reality-based. Thus, *rationality* is defined as that which helps people to achieve their basic goals and purposes, is logical (nonabsolutist), and is empirically consistent with reality. Conversely, *irrationality* refers to that which prevents people from achieving their basic goals and purposes, is illogical (especially, dogmatic and "musturbatory"), and is empirically inconsistent with reality.

THE *ABC* FRAMEWORK

The *ABC* framework is the cornerstone of RET practice. The *A* in this framework stands for an *activating event*, which may be either external or internal to your client. When *A* refers to an external event, we can say that it actually occurred if descriptions of it can be confirmed as accurate by neutral observers (i.e., the principle of confirmable reality). Some RET therapists prefer to include only confirmable events or events imagined by the client under *A*, grouping all cognitive activity (including inferences) under *B*. In this primer, however, *A* will also stand for your client's inferences or interpretations about the activating event.

B stands for *beliefs*. These are evaluative cognitions or constructed views of the world that are either rigid or flexible. When these beliefs are rigid, they are called *irrational beliefs* and take the form of musts, absolute shoulds, have to's, got to's, and so forth. When your clients adhere to rigid premises, they will also tend to draw irrational conclusions on the basis of them. These irrational conclusions take the following forms:

1. Awfulizing: Your clients will express the belief that a situation is more than 100 percent bad, worse than it absolutely should be.

2. I-can't-stand-it-itis (low frustration tolerance): Your clients will say they cannot envision being able to endure situations or having any happiness at all if what they demand must not exist actually exists.

3. Damnation: Your clients will tend to be excessively critical of self, others, and/or life conditions.

4. Always-and-never thinking: Your clients will insist on absolutes (e.g., that they will *always* fail or *never* be approved of by significant others).

When your clients' beliefs are flexible, they are called *rational beliefs*. Rational beliefs often take the form of desires, wishes, wants, and preferences. These beliefs do not escalate into dogmatic musts, shoulds, oughts, and so on. When your clients adhere to such flexible premises, they will tend to draw rational conclusions from them. These conclusions take the following forms:

1. Moderate evaluations of badness: Your clients will conclude "It's bad, but it's not terrible" rather than "It's awful" when faced with a negative activating event.

2. Statements of toleration: Your clients will express tolerant views. They may say, for example, "I don't like it, but I can bear it."

3. Acceptance of fallibility: Your clients will accept themselves and others as fallible human beings who cannot legitimately be given a single global rating. They will also accept the world and life conditions as being complex—composed of good, bad, and neutral elements.

4. Flexible thinking with respect to the occurrence of events: Your clients will refrain from thinking that something will always or never happen. Rather, they will realize that most events in the universe can be placed along a continuum from occurring very rarely to occurring very frequently.

C in the ABC framework stands for emotional and behavioral *consequences* of your clients' beliefs about A. The C's that follow from rigid, irrational beliefs about negative A's will be disturbed and are called *inappropriate negative consequences*, whereas the C's that follow from flexible, rational beliefs about negative A's will be nondisturbed and are termed *appropriate negative consequences* (Crawford & Ellis, 1989).

One type of consequence involves the emotions associated with an activating event. These emotions are of two types. The first, *inappropriate negative emotions*, are inappropriate for any one or more of the following reasons:

1. They lead to the experience of a great deal of psychic pain and discomfort.

2. They motivate one to engage in self-defeating behavior.

3. They prevent one from carrying out behavior necessary to reach one's goals.

Conversely, *appropriate negative emotions* are appropriate for any one or more of the following reasons:

1. They alert one that one's goals are being blocked but do not immobilize one.

2. They motivate one to engage in self-enhancing behavior.

3. They encourage the successful execution of behavior necessary to reach one's goals.

Table 1 outlines some of the major emotional problems for which clients seek therapy and lists their constructive alternatives. Included are both the type of belief and the inferences most commonly associated with each of these emotions.

TABLE 1 Inappropriate and Appropriate Negative Emotions and Their Cognitive Correlates

Inference Related to Personal Domain	Type of Belief	Emotion	Appropriateness of Emotion
Threat or danger	Irrational	Anxiety	Inappropriate
	Rational	Concern	Appropriate
Loss (with implications for future); failure	Irrational	Depression	Inappropriate
	Rational	Sadness	Appropriate
Breaking of personal rule (other or self); other threatens self; frustration	Irrational	Damning anger	Inappropriate
	Rational	Nondamning anger (or annoyance)	Appropriate
Breaking of own moral code	Irrational	Guilt	Inappropriate
	Rational	Remorse	Appropriate
Other betrays self (self nondeserving)	Irrational	Hurt	Inappropriate
	Rational	Disappointment	Appropriate
Threat to desired exclusive relationship	Irrational	Morbid jealousy	Inappropriate
	Rational	Nonmorbid jealousy	Appropriate
Personal weakness revealed publicly	Irrational	Shame	Inappropriate
	Rational	Regret	Appropriate

Note. An *inference* is an interpretation, whether accurate or inaccurate, that goes beyond observable reality but that gives meaning to it. *Personal domain* refers to those tangible or intangible objects in which a person has an involvement (Beck, 1976). Rational-emotive theory distinguishes between ego and comfort aspects of the personal domain, although these aspects frequently interact.

THREE BASIC MUSTS

Although your clients will express their irrational beliefs in personally distinctive terms, you may find it helpful to consider these individualistic beliefs to be variations of three basic *musts*. These involve the following types of demands:

1. Demands about self: This must is frequently revealed in statements such as "I must do well and be approved by significant others, and if I'm not, then it's awful" or "I can't stand it, and I am a damnable person to some degree when I am not loved or when I do not do well." Beliefs based on this must often lead to anxiety, depression, shame, and guilt.

2. Demands about others: This must is often expressed in statements like "You must treat me well and justly, and it's awful and I can't bear it when you don't" or "You are damnable when you don't treat me well, and you deserve to be punished for doing what you must not do." Beliefs based on this must are associated with feelings of anger and rage, as well as with passive-aggressiveness and acts of violence.

3. Demands about the world/life conditions: This must often takes the form of the belief that "Life conditions under which I live must absolutely be the way I want them to be, and if they are not, it's terrible, I can't stand it, poor me." Such beliefs are associated with feelings of self-pity and hurt, as well as with problems of self-discipline (e.g., procrastination or addictive behavior).

INTERACTION OF *A, B,* and *C*

In our simplified presentation of the *ABC* framework, it is assumed that activating events and/or inferences about these events (*A's*) engage evaluative beliefs (*B's*), which in turn lead to feelings and behaviors (*C's*). In reality, *A, B,* and *C* frequently interact in quite complex ways (Ellis, 1985a).

For example, your clients' dogmatic beliefs at B will often lead them to reach an overly negative inference at A or to focus on particular features of A that they might not attend to if they had more rational beliefs. Thus, if your clients dogmatically believe that they must not be socially rejected, they may overestimate the likelihood of being rejected and focus on the negative statements others make about them to the exclusion of more neutral or positive statements. In similar fashion, having certain feelings (C's), such as depression, may cause clients to evaluate events (B's) in an overly negative way. Furthermore, being in a certain context at A may influence your clients to make certain evaluations (B's) that they might not make if they were in another context. For example, being in a dark, unfamiliar room might invoke more anxiety-creating beliefs than being in a well-lit, familiar room.

Because a full analysis of the ways in which A, B, and C interact is beyond the scope of this discussion, we suggest that you consult the texts listed at the end of this primer for further information.

TWO BASIC BIOLOGICAL TENDENCIES

Albert Ellis has made the important point that people very easily tend to escalate their desires into absolute musts, particularly when those desires are strong (Ellis, 1976). The fact that we seem to do this so easily and frequently has led Ellis to conclude that this pattern constitutes a basic biological tendency in most, if not all, humans. Although Ellis does acknowledge that social influences also have an effect in this regard, he has noted that "even if everybody had had the most rational upbringing, virtually all humans would often irrationally escalate their individual and social preferences into absolute demands on (a) themselves, (b) other people, and (c) the universe around them" (Ellis, 1984a, p. 20).

As Ellis points out, however, humans have a second basic biological tendency: the power of choice and the ability to identify, challenge, and change irrational thinking. So, although the tendency to think irrationally may in part have a strong biological component, we are not slaves to this tendency. We can strive to overcome it by repeatedly working to change our irrational beliefs.

THEORY OF CHANGE IN RET

Given that we are not slaves to our tendency to think irrationally, RET argues that we can change, particularly if we internalize three major insights:

1. Past or present activating events do not "cause" disturbed emotional and behavioral consequences. Rather, our belief systems about these activating events largely create our disturbed feelings and behaviors.

2. Irrespective of how we have disturbed ourselves in the past, we now upset ourselves chiefly because we keep reindoctrinating ourselves with our irrational beliefs.

3. Because we are human and very easily (and to some degree naturally) tend to disturb ourselves and because we find it easy to cling to our self-defeating thoughts, feelings, and actions, we can overcome our disturbances in the long run mainly by working hard and repeatedly to dispute our irrational beliefs and the effects of these beliefs.

OVERVIEW OF RET THEORY

RET is a structured approach to emotional problem solving in which the therapist adopts an active-directive approach to helping clients solve their own problems. RET is multimodal in nature in that therapists use and encourage their clients to use a variety of cognitive, imaginal, behavioral, and emotive-evocative techniques to facilitate therapeutic change. Rational-emotive therapists consider that the bulk of therapeutic change is achieved by clients in their daily lives rather than inside therapy sessions. As such, therapists routinely encourage their clients to carry out homework assignments that are individually designed to help them put into practice what they have learned within therapy sessions.

Part II

PRACTICE

The following discussion provides a brief overview of the basic RET treatment process, as summarized in Table 2. For the purpose of illustration, we assume that you will be dealing with your client's emotional problems one at a time. We thus restrict ourselves to specifying the treatment process as it pertains to a given client problem. Once again, it is important to point out that the actual clinical situation may be far more complex than is indicated in this brief analysis.

Before beginning the treatment process outlined in the following pages, it is important first to greet the client and settle any practical issues that may be of concern (e.g., fees, scheduling of appointments, etc.).

TABLE 2 The Rational-Emotive Treatment Sequence

Step 1:   Ask for a Problem

Step 2:   Define and Agree upon the Target Problem

Step 3:   Assess *C*

Step 4:   Assess *A*

Step 5:   Identify and Assess Any Secondary Emotional Problems

Step 6:   Teach the *B-C* Connection

Step 7:   Assess Beliefs

Step 8:   Connect Irrational Beliefs and *C*

Step 9:   Dispute Irrational Beliefs

Step 10: Prepare Your Client to Deepen Conviction in Rational Beliefs

Step 11: Encourage Your Client to Put New Learning into Practice

Step 12: Check Homework Assignments

Step 13: Facilitate the Working-through Process

Note. A = activating event; *B* = belief; *C* = emotional and behavioral consequences

Step 1 | Ask for a Problem

After you discuss the necessary practicalities, we suggest that you establish the problem-solving orientation of RET immediately by asking your client what problem she would like to discuss first. Establishing the *target problem* communicates a number of messages to the client. First, it emphasizes that you are both there to get a job done (i.e., to help the client overcome her emotional problems). Second, it illustrates that RET is an efficient and focused approach to emotional problem solving. Third, it indicates that, as a therapist, you are going to be active and direct your client immediately to a discussion of her problems.

Client choice versus client's most serious problem

You can adopt two basic strategies when asking your client to focus on a target problem. In the first case, you ask your client to choose the issue ("What would you like to work on first?"). The client's selection may or may not be her most serious problem. The second strategy is to ask your client to start with her most serious problem ("What are you most bothered about in your life right now?").

When your client does not identify a target problem

What can you do if your client does not identify a problem to address? (This situation often arises when your "client" is a fellow mental health practitioner with whom you are conducting a peer counseling session during RET training.) First, let your client know that she does not have to choose a serious problem. Tell her that it is perfectly in order to start the process with an issue that is impeding her in some slight way. Remind her that there is always something we can work on because human beings usually operate at a less than optimal level of functioning. Encourage your client to identify *feelings* or *behaviors* she would like to decrease or increase.

Another, more indirect, way of helping your client disclose a target problem is to ask what she would like to achieve from therapy. When your client articulates a goal, you could then ask for ways in which she is presently not achieving this goal. This may well lead to a discussion of feelings and/or behaviors that your client identifies as impediments. You could then explore these impediments further without necessarily labeling them as problems. The word *problem* serves to discourage some clients from becoming engaged in a problem-focused therapy such as RET. If this is the case, use a term that is more acceptable.

Step 2 | Define and Agree upon the Target Problem

The nature of your client's problem is often obvious after an initial discussion. If this is the case, you may proceed to assess the problem (Steps 3, 4, and 5). However, when your client's target problem is unclear, or when he has disclosed a number of problems, the two of you should come to an agreement as to the nature of the problem and/or which problem to work on first.

Arriving at a common understanding of the problem and agreeing to work on it is an important step in RET in that it strengthens the therapeutic alliance. Doing so enables you and your client to work as a team and helps your client to feel understood and have confidence that you know what you are doing.

Distinguish between an emotional and a practical problem

As Bard (1980) has noted, RET is a method of psychotherapy that helps clients overcome their *emotional* problems and not their *practical* difficulties. Of course, clients often have emotional problems about their practical problems, and these may well become the focus of therapeutic exploration. Also, as clients' emotional problems (e.g., anxiety) are addressed, their practical problems (e.g., lack of finances) may also be solved, even though the therapeutic exploration does not expressly deal with such issues (Ellis, 1985b). In any case, it is important to help your client to understand this distinction.

Target inappropriate but not appropriate negative emotions

In Part I, we distinguished between inappropriate and appropriate negative emotions. Do not encourage your client to change appropriate negative emotions; these healthy reactions to negative life events will help your client (a) adjust positively to the negative A, (b) cope better with that A, or (c) change the A in more constructive ways. However, do target for change inappropriate negative emotions (i.e., those that stem from irrational beliefs). Help your client to understand the difference between these two types of negative emotions. The question "How is this a problem for you?" will often lead to a useful discussion and help you and your client to identify and define a "real" emotional problem.

Operationalize vague problems

When your client discusses his target problem in vague or confusing terms, it is important that you help him operationalize the problem. For example, if your client says, "My wife is a pain in the ass," help him specify what this statement means in operational terms (e.g., "What is it your wife does that leads you to conclude that she is a pain in the ass, and how do you feel when she acts this way?").

If you do this, you will find that you are beginning to formulate the problem in *ABC* terms. The practical problem (or A) is the wife's behavior, which makes her "a pain in the ass"; the emotional problem (or C) is the disturbed, inappropriate emotion your client feels when his wife acts poorly.

Focus on helping your client change C, not A

A common difficulty you may face at this point is that your client may wish to change A rather than the feelings (C) about A. As noted earlier, changing the A is a practical solution; changing the C is the emotional solution. If you encounter this difficulty, you can use a number of strategies to encourage your client to change C before attempting to change A:

1. You can help your client to see that he can change A more effectively if he is not emotionally disturbed about the problems at C.

2. It may be that your client already knows how to change *A* but cannot presently do so. If this is the case, it is important to help him understand that the reason he cannot use his productive problem-solving strategies to change *A* probably concerns the fact that he is emotionally disturbed about *A*.

3. If your client does not yet have productive problem-solving strategies in his repertoire to change *A*, you can often encourage him to focus on his problems at *C* by showing him that he will learn such strategies if he is not emotionally disturbed about *A*.

When you still have not identified a problem

If at this stage you still have not reached an agreement with your client concerning the nature of the problem, you can suggest that he keep a *problem diary.* Encourage your client to monitor his disturbed feelings during the following week and suggest that he make written notes of what these feelings are, as well as when and where he experiences them.

Be specific in assessing the target problem

In defining and agreeing upon the target problem, it is important that you be as specific as you can. Your client experiences his emotional problem and holds related irrational beliefs in specific contexts and, as such, being specific will help you to obtain reliable and valid data about *A*, *B*, and *C*. Giving your client a plausible rationale for specificity is a good idea, especially if he tends to discuss his target problem in vague terms. Help him to understand that being specific about the problem will help him deal more constructively with it in the situations about which he is disturbed. A good way of modeling specificity for your client is to ask for a recent or typical example of the target problem (e.g., "When is the last time *A* happened?").

If, after repeated attempts, your client is still unable to provide you with a specific example of the target problem, this may be evidence that he has a secondary emotional problem about his primary emotional problem. If you suspect this is the case, don't assume that you are correct; test your hypothesis. (See Step 5 for further discussion of this point.)

Step 3 | Assess C

At this stage, you may assess either *C* or *A*, depending on which element of the target problem your client raises first. For the purpose of this discussion, we will first consider issues involved in the assessment of *C*.

Check again for an inappropriate negative emotion

In assessing *C*, remember that your client's emotional problem will be an inappropriate (disturbed) negative emotion, not an appropriate (nondisturbed) negative emotion. As noted earlier, an inappropriate negative emotion differs from an appropriate negative emotion in that the former usually involves a great deal of emotional pain, motivates one to behave in a self-defeating manner, and blocks one from achieving one's goals.

Table 1 in Part I lists words used in RET theory to distinguish between these two types of negative emotion. Although these distinctions are important, you should not necessarily expect your client to use this terminology in the same way that you do. For example, your client may talk about *anxiety* when she is actually experiencing *concern*, or vice versa (Dryden, 1986). It is important that you identify an inappropriate negative emotion and that you and your client use the same language when referring to it. You may either encourage your client to adopt the RET terminology of emotion, or you may choose to adopt the client's use of feeling language. Whatever course you take, be consistent in your vocabulary throughout therapy.

Focus on an emotional C

We recognize that *C* may be either emotional or behavioral. However, because dysfunctional behaviors are often

19

defensive and exist to help clients avoid experiencing certain inappropriate negative emotions, we encourage you to avoid dealing with inappropriate negative behaviors and focus instead on inappropriate negative emotions. Thus, if your client wishes to stop smoking, regard smoking as a defensive behavior and encourage her to identify the problematic emotions she might experience were she to refrain from smoking. We suggest that you also adopt this strategy if your client identifies her problem as being procrastination or some other kind of avoidance behavior.

Clarify C

If your client identifies a vague C, there are a number of specific techniques you can use to clarify its nature. For example, you can use imagery methods or Gestalt exercises like the empty chair technique (see Passons, 1975) or Gendlin's (1978) focusing technique. When Ellis's clients experience difficulty in identifying a specific emotion, he encourages them to "Take a wild guess," a method that yields surprisingly useful information about C.

Understand that frustration is an A, not a C

Your client may talk about feeling frustrated at C. Some RET therapists regard frustration to be an activating event (A) rather than a feeling (Trexler, 1976). As a C, frustration in RET theory is usually regarded as an appropriate negative emotion experienced by your client when her goals are blocked. However, when your client says that she feels frustrated, it is possible that she is referring to an inappropriate negative emotion. One way of telling whether your client's frustration is appropriate or inappropriate is to ask whether or not the feeling is bearable. If your client says the feeling is unbearable, then it may well be that she is experiencing an inappropriate negative emotion that should be targeted for change.

Consider your client's motivation to change C

Sometimes a client will experience inappropriate, disturbed negative emotions that she is not motivated to change. This lack of motivation can result when your client does not recognize the destructive nature of the emotion she is experiencing. This situation occurs most frequently in the case of anger; it also sometimes happens in the case of guilt and depression. We therefore recommend that you assess your client's understanding of the dysfunctionality or self-defeating nature of the target emotion (C). If your client does not understand why her emotion is inappropriate, spend as much time as necessary helping her comprehend this point. Basically, this can be accomplished in three steps:

1. Help your client to assess the consequences of the inappropriate negative emotion. What happens when she feels this way? Does she act constructively? Does she act self-defeatingly? Does she stop herself from acting appropriately?

2. Point out that the goal is to replace the inappropriate emotion with the corresponding appropriate emotion. Making this point may be difficult, especially if your client has rigid ideas about the ways she is supposed to feel. However, if provided with appropriate models, your client will usually be able to understand that one can experience the appropriate emotion in any given situation.

3. Finally, assess what the consequences would be if your client felt the corresponding appropriate emotion in the same situation. Because she has probably not considered such a change, help her to imagine how she would act and how the outcome would be different if she did experience the appropriate emotion in the context of the activating event. Compare the outcomes of both inappropriate and appropriate emotions. Your client will usually comprehend the advantages of the appropriate emotion, and this understanding will increase her motivation to change C.

Avoid pitfalls in assessing C

There are a number of pitfalls in assessing your client's problematic emotions at C. The following suggestions will help you avoid them:

1. Do not ask questions that reinforce the assumption
   that *A* causes *C*. Novice RET therapists frequently ask
   their clients, "How does the situation make you feel?"
   An alternative question that does not imply *A* causes *C*
   is "How do you feel about the situation?"

2. Do not accept vague descriptions of feelings, such as
   "bad," "upset," "miserable," and so forth. When your
   client uses vague terms, help her clarify exactly what
   she feels at *C*. (See Table 1 in Part I for discriminations
   among negative emotions.) Also, do not accept
   statements such as "I feel trapped" or "I feel rejected" as
   descriptions of emotions occurring at *C*. Recognize that
   we do not have a feeling called *trapped* or *rejected*.
   These terms refer to combinations of *A*, *B*, and *C*
   factors, and it is important to distinguish among these
   three and ensure that your client's *C* statements
   actually do refer to emotions. For example, if your client
   says, "I feel rejected," help her to recognize that she may
   have been rejected at *A*. Then ask how she felt about
   the rejection at point *C* (e.g., "hurt," "ashamed," etc.).

Step 4 | Assess *A*

If you have chosen first to assess *C*, your next step will be to assess *A*. As noted earlier, *A* refers to activating events that may be regarded as confirmable reality (i.e., your client's descriptions of *A* can be confirmed as accurate by neutral observers). However, in this book *A* will also stand for your client's inferences or interpretations about the activating event.

Be specific in assessing *A*

As with assessments of *C*, be as specific as you can when you assess *A*. For instance, ask for the last time *A* occurred, a typical example of *A*, or the most relevant example your client can recall.

Identify the part of *A* that triggers *B*

While you are assessing *A*, help your client to identify the most relevant part of *A* (i.e., the part that triggers his irrational belief at *B*). Sometimes identifying this trigger can be complicated by inferences your client makes about the situation. You can pinpoint the most important of these by using *inference chaining*, a technique that helps you clarify how your client's inferences are linked.

For example, imagine a client who is anxious at point *C*. Your first inquiry concerning what he is anxious about reveals that he is due to give a class presentation. Now your task is to find out what it is about giving a class presentation that is anxiety-provoking in your client's mind:

Therapist: What is it about giving the presentation that you are anxious about?

Client: Well, I may not do a very good job.

Therapist: Let's assume for the moment that you
             don't. What's anxiety-provoking in
             your mind about that?

Client: Well, if I don't do a good job in class,
             then my teacher will give me a poor
             grade.

Therapist: Let's assume that as well. What would
             you be anxious about there?

Client: That I might flunk the course.

Therapist: And if you did?

Client: Oh, my God, I couldn't face my father.

Therapist: If you told your father that you had
             failed, what would be anxiety-
             provoking about that in your
             mind?

Client: I can just see my father now—he
             would be devastated.

Therapist: And how would you feel if that
             happened?

Client: Oh, my God, that would be terrible. I
             really couldn't stand to see my father
             cry—I'd feel so very sorry for him.

Your client initially identified giving the class presentation as the A. However, inference chaining has uncovered
your client's fearful anticipation of his father's devastation upon hearing of the client's presumed failure. To test
whether this aspect of A is in fact the most relevant factor
in your client's emotional problem, you could write down
the inference chain and review it with your client, asking
him to identify which point he feels is most important. Another way of finding out whether the new aspect of A is central is to manipulate A and check your client's responses at
C. For example, you might say to your client, "Let's suppose
you told your father you flunked the course, and he wasn't
devastated—in fact, he coped quite well with the news.

Would that have any impact on your anxiety about giving the class presentation?" If the client states that it would, you may be more confident that you have assessed the problem correctly. If your client states that he would still be anxious, then it is clear that the prospect of seeing his father's distress (at A) is not the most important factor in the anxiety problem.

Once you have helped your client establish the most relevant aspect of A, it is important to reassess any changes in his feelings at C since the initial analysis of the problem. For example, assuming that the new aspect of A in the case above is indeed the central factor, it would be important to encourage your client to see that his anxiety is more closely associated with the overwhelming pity he would feel at C for his father than with any general fears of failure he might have. In terms of treatment, then, two directions would be possible: The first would involve focusing on the client's feelings of anxiety at C about the future prospect of his father's emotional devastation. Alternatively, you could ask your client to assume that the new A (the father's devastation) had already taken place, then deal with the feelings of pity that would presumably occur at C.

Remember that A can refer to many things

It is important to keep in mind that, in our view, A might be a thought, an inference, an image, a sensation, or a behavior, as well as an event that can be confirmed by neutral observers. Therefore, your client's feelings at C may also serve as an A. For example, your client may feel guilty at C. This guilt may serve as a new A, and your client may feel ashamed (a new C) about feeling guilty. Your client may indeed have such a secondary emotional problem about a primary emotional problem, although this is not always the case. Determining the existence of secondary emotional problems requires careful and open-minded assessment (see Step 5).

Assume temporarily that A is true

When you assess A, you may discover that your client's most relevant A is a clear distortion of reality. If this is the case, you may be tempted to dispute A. Resist this temptation. Rather, at this stage you should encourage your client to assume temporarily that *A* is correct. For example, in the case previously described, it is not important to determine whether or not the client's father would truly be devastated by news of the client's failure. What is important is that you encourage your client to assume that *A* is correct in order to help him identify more accurately the irrational beliefs about the *A* that have led to his feelings at *C*.

Avoid pitfalls in assessing *A*

There are a number of pitfalls to avoid in assessing *A*. The following suggestions can help you avoid them:

1. Do not obtain too much detail about *A*. Allowing your client to talk at length about *A* can discourage you both from retaining a problem-solving approach to overcoming emotional difficulties. If your client does provide too much detail, try to abstract the salient theme or summarize what you understand to be the major aspect of *A*. Interrupt your client tactfully and reestablish a specific focus. For example, you could say, "I think you may be giving me more detail than I require. What was it about the situation that you were most upset about?"

2. Discourage your client from describing *A* in vague terms. As is the case in assessing *C*, get as clear and specific an example of *A* as you can. (An example of a vague *A* would be the statement "My wife reacted negatively to me." In contrast, a specific *A* would be "My wife called me a jerk when I told her I cried at the movie last night.")

3. Discourage your client from talking about several *A*'s at one time. In RET, it is important for you to work on one *A* at a time; therefore, encourage your client to deal with the *A* he considers to best illustrate the context in which he makes himself disturbed. Explain that you will deal with the other *A*'s at a later date.

When you still have not identified *A*

If at this stage your client has still not identified a clear *A*, encourage him to keep a diary during the time before his next session. In this diary, he can record examples of activating events about which he makes himself disturbed.

Agree on goals

Earlier, we stressed that it is important for you and your client to develop a common understanding of the target problem. We also recommend that you develop a similar understanding concerning your client's goals for change—and for a similar reason. Specifically, doing so facilitates a therapeutic alliance between you and your client.

When to agree on goals

There are two main times when you will want to assess your client's goals for change. The first is when you define and agree upon your client's target problem (Step 2). We suggest that, at this early point, you help your client set a goal in line with the problem as initially assessed. For example, if your client's problem relates to being overweight, an initial goal would be for him to achieve and maintain a specific target weight.

However, you may wish to reconsider your client's goal at the assessment stage (Steps 3, 4, and 5). For example, suppose that after you have agreed that your client's goal is to achieve and maintain a specific weight, your assessment reveals that he becomes anxious and overeats when he is bored. At this point, your client's reformulated goal might concern his ability to deal more appropriately with the feeling of boredom so that he does not use the inappropriate coping strategy of overeating. Thus, you may encourage your client to feel concerned (rather than anxious) about being bored and to use that feeling of concern to deal with boredom in more constructive ways. In general, then, encourage your client to select as a goal an appropriate negative emotion and to understand why such an emotion is a realistic and constructive response to a negative activating event at *A*.

Help your client take a long-term perspective

When discussing goals with your client, keep in mind the distinction between *long-term goals* and *short-term goals*. Your client may choose a short-term goal that may in the long term be self-defeating and therefore irrational (e.g., in the case of an anorexic client, the desire to lose more weight). Help the client adopt a broader perspective and obtain his commitment to work towards productive long-term goals.

Avoid pitfalls when agreeing on goals

Several pitfalls need to be avoided when establishing goals. The following suggestions will be helpful in doing so:

1. Do not accept your client's goal statements when they express the wish to experience less of an inappropriate negative emotion (e.g., "I want to feel less anxious" or "I want to feel less guilty"). According to rational-emotive theory, the presence of an inappropriate negative emotion (e.g., anxiety or guilt) indicates that your client is holding an irrational belief. As such, you are advised to help your client distinguish between the inappropriate negative emotion in question and its appropriate parallel emotion. Encourage your client to set the latter emotion as his goal. He can therefore choose to feel concerned instead of anxious and sorry instead of guilty or self-downing.

2. Do not accept goals indicating that your client wishes to feel neutral, indifferent, or calm about events about which it would be rational to feel an appropriate negative emotion. Emotions indicating indifference (e.g., calmness when an unfortunate event occurs) mean that your client does not have a rational belief about the event in question, whereas in reality he probably would prefer that the event not happen. If you go along with your client's goal to feel calm or indifferent about a negative event, you will encourage him to deny the existence of his desires rather than to think rationally.

3. For similar reasons, do not accept your client's goal to experience positive feelings about a negative A. It is unrealistic for your client to feel happy, for example, when he is faced with a negative life event that he would prefer not to encounter (e.g., a loss or a failure). If you accept your client's goals to feel positive about a

negative event, you will encourage him to believe that it is good that the negative *A* occurred. By doing this, you will once again be discouraging your client from thinking rationally. To reiterate an earlier point, when you encourage your client to experience appropriate negative feelings in the face of negative life events, you help him to come to terms with or change his situation.

4. Finally, do not accept vague goals (e.g., "I want to be happy"). The more specific you can encourage your client to be in setting goals, the more he will be motivated to do the hard work of changing his irrational beliefs in the service of achieving these goals.

Step 5 | Identify and Assess Any Secondary Emotional Problems

Clients frequently have secondary emotional problems about their primary emotional problems. If your client's primary problem is anxiety, you may ask "How do you feel about feeling anxious?" to determine whether or not your client does in fact have a secondary emotional problem about the primary problem of anxiety.

Know when to work on the secondary emotional problem first

We suggest that you first focus attention on your client's secondary problem if any of the following three conditions are met:

1. If your client's secondary problem interferes significantly with the work you are trying to do on her primary problem. Such interference might take place in either the session or the client's outside life.

2. If, from a clinical perspective, the secondary problem is the more important of the two.

3. If your client can see the sense of working on her secondary emotional problem first.

You may need to present a plausible rationale for starting with the secondary problem first. If, after you have presented your rationale, your client still wishes to work on her primary problem first, then do so. To do otherwise may threaten the productive therapeutic alliance you have by now established.

31

Check for an emotional problem about an appropriate negative emotion

When you have assessed your client's *stated* primary problem, you may decide that she is in fact experiencing an appropriate negative emotion (e.g., sadness in response to an important loss). If so, check to see whether your client has a problem with this appropriate emotion. For example, your client may feel ashamed about feeling sad. If this is the case, work to reach an agreement that the secondary emotional problem (shame) will be the client's target problem and proceed to carry out an assessment of this agreed-upon problem.

Assess the presence of shame

As noted earlier, if your client is reluctant to disclose that she has an emotional problem, she may feel ashamed about having the problem or about disclosing it to a therapist. When you suspect that this might be the case, ask your client how she would feel if she did have an emotional problem about the activating event you are discussing. If she says that she would feel ashamed, agree with your client to work on shame as the target problem before encouraging her to disclose the original problem she had in mind.

Step 6 | Teach the *B-C* Connection

By now you will have assessed the *A* and *C* elements of your client's primary or secondary problem. The next step is to teach the *B-C connection*—the notion that your client's emotional problem is largely determined by his beliefs rather than by the activating event you have already assessed. Carrying out this step is critical. Unless your client understands that his emotional problem is determined by his beliefs, he will not understand why you would want to assess his beliefs during the next step of the treatment process. Using an example unrelated to your client's problem can often help to explain the concept. Other exercises and metaphors to help teach the idea are detailed in the RET texts listed at the end of this book (e.g., Dryden, 1987; Ellis & Dryden, 1987; Walen et al., 1980).

Step 7 | Assess Beliefs

While assessing *B*, keep clear in your mind the distinction between your client's rational and irrational beliefs, and help your client understand the difference between these two kinds of thinking.

Assess both premise and derivative forms

In Part I, we argued that your client's beliefs can be divided into a premise and certain derivatives from this premise. At this stage of the process, you should carefully assess your client's irrational beliefs. As you do so, assess both the premise form (dogmatic musts, absolute shoulds, have to's, oughts, etc.) and the four main derivatives from the premise: (a) awfulizing, (b) I-can't-stand-it-itis, (c) damnation, and (d) always-and-never thinking. As you do this, you can either teach and use the RET terms for these processes or use your client's own language, ensuring that her terms accurately reflect irrational beliefs. Base your decision on your client's feedback concerning which of these strategies will be most useful.

Remember the three basic musts

While assessing your client's irrational beliefs, keep in mind the three basic musts outlined in Part I: demands about self, demands about others, and demands about the world/life conditions.

Distinguish between absolute shoulds and other shoulds

While you are assessing the premise form of your client's irrational beliefs, she may use the word *should*. This word has several different meanings in the English language. Most expressions of the word *should* are unrelated to your client's emotional problems. These include shoulds of preference (e.g., "You *should* preferably treat your children with respect"); empirical shoulds (e.g., "When two parts of hydrogen and one part of oxygen are mixed, you *should* get water"); and shoulds of recommendation ("You *should* go see that excellent play at the local theater").

Rational-emotive theory hypothesizes that only *absolute shoulds* are related to emotional disturbance. If your client finds the different meanings confusing, it may be helpful to substitute the word *must* in cases where an irrational belief in its premise form may be operative. (Compare, for instance, "I *should* be admired by my colleagues" and "I *must* be admired by my colleagues.") It is Ellis's and our clinical experience that the word *must* conveys the meaning of absolute demanding better than the word *should*. In particular, help your client distinguish between absolute shoulds and shoulds of preference.

Use questions in assessing irrational beliefs

When you assess your client's irrational beliefs, use questions. A standard question RET therapists frequently ask is "What were you telling yourself about *A* to make yourself disturbed at *C?*" This type of *open-ended question* has both advantages and disadvantages. The main advantage in using this type of inquiry is that you are unlikely to put words in your client's mouth concerning the content of her belief. The main disadvantage is that your client will be unlikely to respond by articulating an irrational belief. Rather, she is most likely to give you further inferences about *A*—ones that may well be less relevant than the one you selected at Step 4.

For example, imagine that your client is particularly anxious that other people will think her a fool if she stammers in public. Asking her, "What were you telling yourself about other people's criticism to make yourself disturbed at *C?*" might yield the response "I thought they wouldn't like me." Note that this thought is in fact an inference and that you still don't know what your client's irrational belief is. In this instance, you would want to help the client understand that her statement does not describe an irrational belief and educate her to look further for her irrational belief about *A*. You can do this by judiciously combining the use of open-ended questions with didactic explanation.

What other kinds of open-ended questions can you use when assessing your client's irrational beliefs? Walen et al. (1980) list a number of possibilities, such as "What was going through your mind?"; "Were you aware of any thoughts in your head?"; "What was on your mind then?"; and "Are you aware of what you were thinking at that moment?" Again, note that your client may not spontaneously disclose irrational beliefs in response to these questions; she may well need further help of a didactic nature.

An alternative to asking open-ended questions at *A* is to ask *theory-driven questions* (i.e., questions that are directly derived from rational-emotive theory). For example, to elicit an answer specifying a must (i.e., a premise), you might ask, "What *demand* were you making about other people's criticism to make yourself disturbed at point *C*?" To assess the presence of a derivative of a must, you might ask, "What kind of person did you think you were for stammering and incurring other people's criticism?"

The advantage of theory-driven questions is that they orient your client to look for her irrational beliefs. The danger is that you may be putting words in your client's mouth and encouraging her to look for irrational beliefs that she may not have. However, you will minimize this danger if you have already established that your client has an inappropriate negative emotion at point *C*.

Step 8 | Connect Irrational Beliefs and C

After you have accurately assessed your client's irrational beliefs in the form of both premise and derivatives, ensure that your client understands the connection between her irrational beliefs and her disturbed emotions at point C before proceeding to dispute these beliefs. Thus, you might say, "Can you understand that as long as you demand that other people must not criticize you, you are bound to make yourself anxious about this happening?" or "Can you see that as long as you believe that you are no good for being regarded by others as a fool, you will be anxious about being criticized?" If your client says yes, you can then attempt to elicit the B-C connection (e.g., "So, in order to change your feeling of anxiety to one of concern, what do you need to change first?"). Eliciting this connection is likely to be more productive than telling your client that such a connection exists. If your client says she understands that she had better change her belief in order to change her feeling, this will indicate that she has grasped the concept. If she does not see the connection, spend time helping her understand it before beginning to dispute her irrational beliefs.

Step 9 | Dispute Irrational Beliefs

After conducting a thorough assessment of the target problem, identifying and assessing any secondary emotional problems, and teaching the *B-C* connection, your next step is to begin disputing your client's irrational beliefs.

Work to achieve the goals of disputing

The major goal of disputing at this stage of the RET treatment process is to encourage your client to understand that his irrational belief is unproductive (i.e., it leads to self-defeating emotions), illogical, and inconsistent with reality, and that the alternative to this belief (i.e., a rational belief) is productive, logical, and consistent with reality.

If you succeed in helping your client achieve such an understanding at this stage, do not assume that his conviction in the rational belief will be strong. Help your client distinguish between *light conviction* and *deep conviction* in a rational belief. Also encourage him to see that, at this stage, even a light conviction in an alternative rational belief (i.e., intellectual understanding) is a sign of progress, albeit insufficient in itself to promote emotional change.

With specific regard to the target problem, the goals of disputing are to help your client understand the following:

1. Musts: There is no evidence in support of the client's absolute demand, whereas evidence does exist for his preferences. (As Ellis often says, "There are most likely no absolute musts in the universe.")

2. Awfulizing: What the client has defined as awful (i.e., 101 percent bad) is magical nonsense and, in reality, all experience lies within a 0–99.9 percent range of badness.

3. I-can't-stand-it-itis: Your client can virtually always stand what he thinks he can't stand and can find some happiness even if bad events at *A* continue.

4. Damnation: Damnation is a concept that is inconsistent with reality and illogical and that will lead your client into emotional trouble. The alternative is for him to accept himself, other people, and the world as fallible and complex—too complex to be given a single global rating.

5. Always-and-never thinking: It is most unlikely that the client will *always* be rejected or *never* succeed in doing well. He is not intrinsically unlovable, nor a total failure.

Much later on in the treatment process (at a point beyond the scope of this primer), your goal will be to help your client internalize a broad range of rational beliefs so that they become part of a general philosophy of rational living.

Use questions during disputing

Let us assume that you are going to dispute your client's irrational belief in the form of a must. The first stage in the disputing sequence is to ask for evidence in support of the must. Standard questions designed to accomplish this include "Where is the evidence that you must under all conditions?"; "Where is the proof?"; "Is it true that you must?"; and "Where is it written that you must?"

Ensure that your client answers the question you have asked. For example, in response to the question "Why must you succeed?" your client might say, "Because it would bring me advantages if I succeed." Note that your client has not addressed himself to the question you actually asked but to a different question, namely, "Why is it *preferable* for you to succeed?" In fact, it is a good idea to anticipate that your client will not immediately provide a correct answer to your question.

According to RET theory, the only correct answer to the question "Why must you succeed?" is "There is no reason why I must succeed, although I would prefer to." If your client gives any other answer, you may need to educate him concerning why his answer is either (a) incorrect with respect to the question you have asked or (b) a correct response to a different question. During this process, use a combination of questions and short didactic explanations until your client gives the correct answer and understands why it is correct.

As a part of this process, again help your client to distinguish between his rational and irrational beliefs. One way of doing this would be to write down the following two questions:

1. Why must you succeed?

2. Why is it preferable but not essential for you to succeed?

Ask your client to answer these questions. It is likely that he will give you the same answer to both. If so, help him to see that the reasons he has given constitute evidence for his rational belief but not for his irrational belief. As we have already stressed, help him to comprehend that the only answer to a question about the existence of musts is, to paraphrase Ellis, "There are probably no absolute musts in the universe."

Be persistent in disputing premise or derivatives

We noted earlier that it is important to dispute your client's irrational beliefs in the form of both his premise (must) and at least one of the four derivatives from that premise (awfulizing, I-can't-stand-it-itis, damnation, or always-and-never thinking). However, if you have decided to dispute the irrational premise, persist until you have shown your client that there is no evidence in support of this premise before beginning to dispute a derivative from the premise.

Switching from premise to derivative (and from derivative to premise) can be confusing for the client. However, if you have persisted in disputing an irrational premise and it becomes clear that your client is not finding this helpful, you may wish to redirect your focus toward a derivative and monitor your client's reactions. Some clients find it easier to understand why these derivatives are irrational than why their musts are irrational.

Use a variety of disputing strategies

There are three basic disputing strategies. It is best to use all three if you can:

1. Focus on illogicality: Your purpose here is to help your client understand why his irrational belief is illogical. Help your client to understand that, just because he wants something to happen, it does not logically follow that it absolutely must happen. Ask the question "Where is the logic?" and stress that your client's must about his preference is magical in nature.

2. Focus on empiricism: Your goal here is to show your client that his musts and associated derivatives from these musts are almost always empirically inconsistent with reality. As such, use questions that ask your client to provide evidence in support of his irrational beliefs (e.g., "Where is the evidence?"). For example, to help your client understand that if there were evidence to support his belief that he must succeed, then he would have to succeed no matter what he believed. If he is not succeeding at present, that fact constitutes evidence that his irrational belief is empirically inconsistent with reality.

3. Focus on pragmatism: The purpose of focusing on the pragmatic consequences of your client's holding irrational beliefs is to show him that, as long as he believes in his irrational musts and their derivatives, he is going to remain disturbed. Ask questions such as "What is believing that you must succeed going to get you other than anxious and depressed?"

Once the irrational belief has been disputed, your client needs to learn to replace it with a new, rational belief. Work together to construct a rational belief that is most adaptive with respect to the A. After you have helped your client construct an alternative rational belief, dispute it logically, empirically, and pragmatically to help your client see that rational beliefs are in fact rational. It is much better for your client to see for himself the evidence that rational beliefs are best than for you to tell him that this is so.

Use a variety of disputing styles

Although many individual variations are possible, four basic styles of disputing your client's irrational beliefs are Socratic, didactic, humorous, and self-disclosing.

Socratic style

When you use the Socratic style of disputing, your main task is to ask questions concerning the illogical, empirically inconsistent, and dysfunctional aspects of your client's irrational beliefs. The purpose of this style is to encourage your client to think for himself rather than to accept your viewpoint just because you have some authority as a therapist. Although this approach depends mainly on questions, brief explanations designed to correct your client's misconceptions may also be included.

Didactic style

Although rational-emotive therapists prefer the Socratic style, asking questions does not always prove productive. If not, you may have to shift to giving more lengthy didactic explanations concerning why an irrational belief is self-defeating and why a rational belief is more productive. Indeed, you will probably have to use didactic explanations to varying degrees with all your clients at some point in the treatment process.

When you use didactic explanations, be sure that your client understands what you have been saying by asking him to paraphrase your point. You might say, for example, "I'm not quite sure whether I'm making myself clear here—perhaps you could put into your own words what you think I've been saying to you." Do not accept without question your client's nonverbal and paraverbal signs of understanding (e.g., head nods, *hmm-hmm's*) as evidence that he has in fact understood you. As one of us (R. D.) often says, "There is no good course without a test!"

Humorous style

With some clients, a productive way of making the point that there is no evidence for irrational beliefs is to use humor or humorous exaggeration. As Walen et al. (1980) note:

> If the client says, "It's really awful that I failed the
> test!" the therapist might respond, "You're right!
> It's not only awful, but I don't see how you're going
> to survive. That's the worst news I've ever heard.
> This is so horrendous that I can't bear to talk
> about it. Let's talk about something else quick."
> Such paradoxical statements frequently point out
> the senselessness of the irrational belief to the
> client and very little further debate may be
> necessary to make the point. (p. 101)

Use humorous exaggeration as a disputing strategy only
if (a) you have established a good relationship with your client, (b) your client has already shown some evidence that
he has a sense of humor, and (c) your humorous interven-
tion is directed at the irrationality of the client's belief and
not at the client as a person.

Self-disclosing style

Another constructive way of disputing your client's irrational beliefs involves therapist self-disclosure. In the *coping model* of self-disclosure, you reveal that (a) you have
experienced a problem similar to your client's, (b) you once
held an irrational belief similar to your client's, and (c) you
changed your belief and no longer have the problem. For
example, one of us (W. D.) has used the personal example of
overcoming anxiety about stammering in public:

> I disclose that I used to believe "I must not
> stammer." I stress that this belief increased rather
> than diminished my anxiety. I then show how I
> disputed this irrational belief by proving to myself
> that there was no evidence to support it, then
> changed it to the following rational belief: "There is
> no reason why I must not stammer. If I stammer, I
> stammer. That's unfortunate, but hardly awful." I
> then describe how I pushed myself to put this
> rational belief into practice while speaking in
> public and finally outline the productive effects
> that I experienced by doing so.

The coping model of self-disclosure contrasts with a
mastery model. In the latter, you disclose the fact that you

have never experienced a problem similar to your client's because you have always thought rationally about the problem at hand. The mastery model tends to accentuate the differences between you and your client and, in our experience, is less productive than the coping model in encouraging your client to challenge his own irrationality. However, some of your clients will not find even the coping model useful. If this is the case, avoid self-disclosure as a disputing strategy and use other strategies instead.

Be creative

The more experience you gain in disputing irrational beliefs, the more you will develop your own individual style of disputing. Thus, you will build up a repertoire of stories, aphorisms, metaphors, and examples to show your clients why their irrational beliefs are indeed irrational and why rational alternatives will promote psychological health.

For example, in working with clients who believe they mustn't experience panic and couldn't stand it if they did, one of us (W. D.) uses a technique called the *Terrorist Dispute:*

> I say, "Let's suppose that your parents have been
> captured by radical terrorists, and these radicals
> will only release your parents if you agree to put up
> with 10 panic attacks. Will you agree to these
> terms?" The client almost always says yes. If so, I
> will then say, "But I thought you couldn't stand the
> experience of panic." The client usually replies,
> "Well, but I would do it in order to save my
> parents." To which I respond, "Yes, but will you do
> it for your own mental health?"

Another creative disputing strategy is what we call the *Friend Dispute*, an approach useful for pointing out the existence of unreasonable self-standards:

> Imagine that your client has failed an important
> test and believes "I must do well, and I am no good
> if I don't." Ask him whether he would condemn his
> best friend for a similar failure in the same way he
> condemns himself. Normally, your client will say

no. If so, point out that he has a different attitude towards his friend than he has towards himself. Suggest that, if he chose to be as compassionate towards himself as he is towards his friend, he would be better able to help himself solve his own emotional problems.

We end this section on disputing irrational beliefs with one piece of advice: Master the basics before trying to be too creative.

Step 10 | Prepare Your Client to Deepen Conviction in Rational Beliefs

Once your client has acknowledged that (a) there is no evidence in support of her irrational beliefs but there is evidence to support her rational beliefs, (b) it would be more logical for her to think rationally, and (c) her rational beliefs will lead her to more productive emotional results than will her irrational beliefs, you are in a position to help her deepen her conviction in her rational beliefs.

Point out why weak conviction will not promote change

Start by helping your client understand why a weak conviction in rational beliefs, although important, is insufficient to promote change. Do this by discussing briefly the rational-emotive view of therapeutic change. Using Socratic questioning and brief didactic explanations (see Step 9), help your client to see that she will strengthen her conviction in her rational beliefs by disputing irrational beliefs and replacing them with their rational alternatives within and between therapy sessions. Also help your client understand that this process will require her to *act* against her irrational beliefs as well as to dispute them cognitively. Establishing this point now will help you later when you encourage your client to put her new learning into practice (Steps 11 and 12) and as you facilitate the working-through process (Step 13).

Deal with the "head-gut" issue

As you help your client to think rationally, she may say something like, "I understand my rational belief will help me achieve my goals, but I don't really believe in it yet." Indeed, you may wish to bring up this point yourself as a prelude to discussing how your client is going to deepen her conviction in her rational belief and weaken her conviction in her irrational one. You might ask, for example, "What do you think you will have to do in order to get your new rational belief into your gut?"

Encourage your client to commit herself to a process of therapeutic change that requires her to dispute her irrational beliefs repeatedly and forcefully, and to practice thinking rationally in relevant life contexts. As described in the following step, this process will involve undertaking a variety of homework assignments.

Step 11 | Encourage Your Client to Put New Learning into Practice

Your client is now ready to put his rational belief into practice. Remind him that the rational emotive theory of change holds that in order to deepen his conviction in his rational belief, he must practice disputing his irrational belief and strengthen his rational belief in situations that are the same or similar to the activating event already assessed. Help your client choose from among a wide variety of homework assignments advocated in RET:

1. Cognitive assignments: These assignments vary in complexity and structure. One typical cognitive assignment would involve having the client practice his disputes by attempting to convince someone else of their rationality. Another might involve having the client rehearse rational self-statements before confronting a problematic activating event. (See Ellis, 1988, and Ellis & Dryden, 1987, for additional examples.)

2. Imagery assignments: These assignments involve your client's deliberate attempts to change an inappropriate negative emotion to an appropriate one, all the while vividly imagining the troublesome activating event. They are particularly helpful when you wish to encourage your client to become confident that he can carry out an in vivo assignment. (See Maultsby & Ellis, 1974, and Walen et al., 1980, for further discussion.)

3. Emotive-evocative assignments: These assignments involve the client's forcefully and vigorously disputing

his irrational beliefs in situations that evoke strong feelings (see Ellis & Dryden, 1987).

4. Behavioral assignments: Sometimes known as *in vivo flooding*, these assignments involve having the client confront straightaway the troublesome situations about which he makes himself disturbed, while simultaneously disputing any irrational beliefs in these contexts. If your client refuses to do this type of assignment, you can encourage him to choose an alternate task that he feels is challenging but not overwhelming. However, try to persuade your client to carry out an assignment that involves at least some discomfort. Whatever behavioral assignment you negotiate with your client, ensure that it is both legal and ethical.

Ensure that homework assignments are relevant

Make sure that homework assignments are relevant to the irrational belief targeted for change and that, if the client carries out these assignments, doing so will help him deepen his conviction in the rational alternative (i.e., his rational belief).

Collaborate with your client

While you are discussing appropriate homework assignments, enlist your client's active collaboration. Ensure that he can see the sense of carrying out the homework assignment; that, if he does so, the experience will help him achieve his goals; and that he has some degree of confidence that he will in fact be able to carry out the assignment. Maximize the chances that your client will complete the assignment by helping him specify when he will do it, in which context, and how frequently.

Be prepared to compromise

An ideal homework assignment will involve the client actively and forcefully in disputing his irrational beliefs in the most relevant context possible. Try to encourage your client to carry out an ideal assignment. If this is not possible, urge him to (a) dispute his irrational beliefs in situations that approximate the most relevant *A* or (b) use imagery and dispute his irrational beliefs while vividly imagining *A*. You may find that, if your client does these less-than-ideal assignments, he will be more likely later on to carry out a more challenging task.

Assess and troubleshoot obstacles

While you are negotiating appropriate homework assignments with your client, help him to specify any obstacles that might serve as impediments. Encourage your client to find possible ways of overcoming these obstacles in advance of carrying out the assignment.

Use homework at different times during therapy

For the purpose of discussion, we have focused on homework assignments that involve your client's strengthening his conviction in rational beliefs. However, you can employ such assignments at any point during the treatment sequence. Specifically, you might encourage your client to carry out homework assignments to help him (a) specify his troublesome emotions at *C*, (b) detect his irrational beliefs at *B*, and (c) identify the most relevant aspect of *A* about which he has made himself disturbed.

You may also employ homework assignments as part of a process in which you educate your client about the *ABC's* of RET. In this case, you could ask your client to read various books (bibliotherapy) or to listen to RET lectures on audiotape. When doing so, choose material that is relevant to your client's problem and that he can readily understand. If no appropriate material is available, you might even create written materials or audiotapes to address your client's particular problem.

Step 12 | Check Homework Assignments

Once you have negotiated a particular homework assignment with your client and she has undertaken it, use the beginning of the next session to check on what she has learned from the experience. If you fail to do this, you show your client that you do not consider homework assignments to be an important ingredient in the process of change. On the contrary, such assignments are central in helping your client achieve her therapeutic goals.

Verify that your client faced A

As noted earlier, clients are prone to develop strategies to avoid A's rather than strategies to confront A's and change C's. Homework assignments are designed to solve emotional problems, not practical problems. Therefore, when you check on your client's experience in carrying out an assignment, make sure she actually faced the A she committed herself to confront. If your client has done this, she will usually report that she first made herself disturbed and then made herself undisturbed in the same situation by using the disputing techniques discussed in therapy. If your client has not done so, point out this fact, deal with any obstacles involved, and encourage her to confront the situation once more and use vigorous disputing to make herself undisturbed in that context. If necessary, model appropriate disputes and encourage your client to rehearse these in the session and before facing the situation in question.

Verify that your client changed *B*

If your client reports a successful experience in carrying out the homework assignment, assess whether her success can be attributed to her (a) changing her irrational belief to its rational alternative, (b) changing either *A* itself or her inferences about *A*, or (c) using distraction techniques. If your client used the latter two methods, acknowledge her efforts but point out that these methods may not be helpful in the long term. Stress that practical solutions or distractions are only palliative because, if one has not learned to change the inappropriate negative emotion associated with the situation, the solution is not a permanent one. If *A's* are unavoidable, the problem will only reassert itself. Once again, encourage the client to face the situation at *A*, but this time elicit her commitment that she will dispute her irrational belief and practice acting on the basis of the new rational belief.

Deal with failure to complete homework

If your client has failed to execute the agreed-upon homework, accept her as a fallible human being and help her identify the reasons she did not carry out the assignment. Use the *ABC* framework to encourage your client to focus on possible irrational beliefs that served to prevent her from carrying out the assignment. Assess in particular whether or not your client held irrational beliefs indicating a low frustration tolerance (e.g., "It was too hard," "I couldn't be bothered," "I shouldn't have to put this much energy into therapy," etc.). If your client holds such beliefs, encourage her to challenge and change them, then reassign the homework.

Step 13 | Facilitate the Working-through Process

For your client to achieve enduring therapeutic change, he needs to challenge and change his irrational beliefs repeatedly and forcefully in relevant contexts at A. In doing so, he will further strengthen his conviction in rational beliefs and continue to weaken his conviction in irrational ones. The purpose of this working-through process is for your client to integrate rational beliefs into his emotional and behavioral repertoire.

Suggest different homework assignments for the same irrational belief

When your client has achieved some success at disputing his irrational belief in relevant situations at A, suggest that he use different homework assignments to encourage change in the same belief. Doing so serves to teach your client that he can use a variety of methods to dispute the target irrational belief, as well as others. In addition, it may help to sustain his interest in the change process.

Discuss the nonlinear model of change

Explain that change is nonlinear and that your client will probably experience some difficulties in sustaining his success at disputing irrational beliefs in a wide variety of contexts. Identify possible setbacks and help your client develop ways of handling these setbacks. In particular, help your client understand and challenge the irrational beliefs that might underpin these relapses.

In addition, explain that change can be evaluated on three major dimensions:

1. Frequency: Does your client make himself disturbed less frequently than he did before?

2. Intensity: When your client makes himself disturbed, does he do so with less intensity than before?

3. Duration: When your client makes himself disturbed, does he do so for shorter periods of time than before?

Encourage your client to keep records of his disturbed emotions at point *C*, using these three criteria for change. At this point, it is also helpful to have your client read *How to Enhance and Maintain Your Rational-Emotive Therapy Gains* (Ellis, 1984b). This booklet contains many useful suggestions to help your client facilitate his own working-through process.

Encourage your client to take responsibility for continued progress

At this stage, you can help your client develop his own homework assignments to change his target belief and to change other irrational beliefs in different situations. Thus, if your client has been successful at disputing an irrational belief about approval in a work-related situation in which he faces criticism, you could encourage him to dispute this belief in other situations in which he may encounter criticism (e.g., with strangers or friends). The more your client develops and carries out his own homework assignments, the more he will begin to serve as his own therapist. This accomplishment is important because, as a rational-emotive therapist, your long-term goal is to encourage your client to internalize the RET model of change and to take responsibility for further progress after therapy has ended.

Part III

CASE EXAMPLE

In the final part of this primer, we present actual case material to illustrate the rational-emotive treatment sequence described in Part II. Although a single case cannot illustrate all the points discussed, we believe that the case chosen does cover the most salient issues. We deliberately selected a case in which the client responded well to RET in order to demonstrate clearly the steps in the RET treatment sequence.

The client, Karen, was referred to me (W. D.) by her general practitioner, whom she had consulted for problems of sleeplessness and general tension. At the time of the referral, Karen was 26 years old and worked as a laboratory technician at a local college. She lived at home with her parents, did not have a partner, but did have several close friends of the same sex whom she had recently been avoiding. Karen had never sought therapy before.

Before beginning the treatment process, I greeted Karen and discovered how she came to be referred to me. Then we discussed her expectations for therapy and agreed on a fee appropriate to her situation.

STEP 1   Ask for a Problem

After dealing with these initial practicalities, I then asked Karen what problem she would like to start with. She said that she had been having trouble sleeping over the past few months and had been avoiding social contact with other people, including her close female friends. She traced the development of these problems back to the dissolution of a relationship with Pete, her fiance, who had left her for another woman 3 months earlier.

I commented that Karen had several problems and suggested that we list them so that we could deal with them one by one. Karen thought that this was a good idea, and we developed the following list:

1. Feelings of hurt about the break-up of my relationship with Pete

2. Avoiding contact with my friends

3. Sleeplessness

4. General tension

I again asked Karen which problem she would like to start with, and she chose avoiding contact with her friends. This issue thus became the target problem of therapy.

STEP 2   Define and Agree upon the Target Problem

I asked Karen to tell me a little more about the problem, and the following dialogue ensued:

Karen: Well, ever since Pete dumped me, I've just not felt like seeing anyone, least of all my friends. Part of me wants to see them because I miss them very much, but another part of me just wants to hibernate.

W. D.:   But let's suppose that you did go to see your friends. What feelings do you think you might experience?

Karen: I'm not sure. I think I would be very
          uncomfortable.

W. D.:   And then what would happen?

Karen: I'd just make some excuse to go home
          again.

W. D.:   So it may be that what you call avoidance
          of social contact with your friends really
          has to do with your avoiding uncom-
          fortable feelings that you think you
          would experience in their presence.

Karen: That seems right.

W. D.:   So why don't we have a closer look at
          those uncomfortable feelings and see what
          they relate to so that you can decide
          whether or not to see your friends from a
          more healthy frame of mind?

Karen: That seems like a good idea.

STEP 3 Assess C

My hypothesis at this point was that Karen's social
avoidance served to help her to avoid negative feelings. I
next moved on to obtain a more precise assessment of
these feelings.

W. D.:   Now, if you were to meet with your close
          friends and remain with them, and you
          really let yourself experience those
          uncomfortable feelings that you
          mentioned, what kind of feelings would
          they be?

Karen: I'm not sure.

W. D.:   Well, close your eyes and see yourself with
          your friends; really try to picture yourself
          and picture them. Try to imagine that you
          are with them right now. What are you
          experiencing?

Karen: (pause) It's funny—I feel anxious.

STEP 4   Assess *A*

As shown in the previous step, Karen had been able to identify the feeling of anxiety as the *C* in the situation. My next step was to use inference chaining to help her define the part of *A* that triggered her anxiety.

> W. D.:   Now open your eyes. You seem surprised to learn that you would feel anxious. What do you think you would be anxious about?

> Karen: Well, when you asked me to picture my friends, I had an image of them disapproving of me.

> W. D.:   For what?

> Karen: Well, it was as if they were thinking, "She can't be up to much if her fiance goes off with another woman."

> W. D.:   Well, we don't know whether or not they would be thinking that, but let's assume for a moment that you were right. What would be anxiety-provoking in your mind if they did think you weren't up to much?

> Karen: Well, it would mean they would look down on me.

> W. D.:   And what would be anxiety-provoking in your mind about that?

> Karen: *(pause)* Just that, that they would look down on me.

> W. D.:   Now, does that seem to explain what those uncomfortable feelings that you mentioned earlier are about?

> Karen: Yes, it does.

> W. D.:   Right, and as we look at it now, with them looking down at you, what feelings go along with that?

> Karen: *(pause)* Shame. Yes, I'd feel very ashamed.

Note that Karen's *C* has changed from anxiety to shame. This frequently happens when the client's disturbed feeling involves anxiety. As shown in Table 1 in Part I, anxiety occurs when the person has an irrational belief about some future threat. When, in the context of exploring the client's *A*, the therapist asks the client to assume that the threat has occurred, the client's feeling changes to reflect this assumption. For example, Karen would be *anxious* about the future prospect that her friends would look down on her but would feel *ashamed* if that event had actually taken place.

During this part of the therapy process, I decided to treat Karen's *C* as shame and thus encouraged her to assume that *A* (her friends looking down on her) had actually occurred. My next task was to encourage her to feel regretful, rather than ashamed, about this situation should it occur.

W. D.:   Now, as long as you feel ashamed in the face of your friends looking down on you, it makes sense for you to avoid them. Can you see that?

Karen: Yes.

W. D.:   But let's see what alternatives you have about handling the situation where they look down on you. I want to stress, however, that we're assuming for the moment that they *would* look down on you. Realistically, they may very well not, but let's assume that they would. What productive feelings could you strive to experience instead of shame?

Karen: To be indifferent towards them?

W. D.:   But is that realistic? Do you think you could ever be indifferent about what your close friends think of you?

Karen: No, I guess not.

W. D.:   What else could you feel instead of shame?

Karen: I'm not sure.

W. D.: How about feeling sorry? My guess is that
        if you felt sorry but not ashamed in the
        face of them looking down on you, you
        wouldn't want to run away and you would
        be in a position to try to persuade them
        that they were wrong to disapprove of you,
        something you couldn't do if you were
        ashamed.

Karen: Yes, that makes sense, but how do I get
        myself to feel sorry rather than ashamed?

STEP 5   Identify and Assess Any Secondary Emotional Problems

From her question at the end of Step 4, it seemed that
Karen was ready to move towards considering how she
could change her feelings of shame to those of sorrow.
Thus, I did not at this point assess the presence of a secondary emotional problem. I did so later on and found that
Karen did not have a secondary emotional problem about
her shame or her social avoidance.

STEP 6   Teach the *B-C* Connection

In the process of teaching the *B-C* connection, I used
an example unrelated to Karen's own problem. By doing so,
I hoped to help her understand with greater objectivity the
distinction between rational and irrational beliefs.

W. D.: The first step to changing your feelings
        from shame to sorrow is to understand
        what determines your feelings. Now, would
        a hundred women of your age all feel
        ashamed if their friends looked down on
        them?

Karen: No, I guess not.

W. D.: Why not?

Karen: Well, people react to the same situation in
        different ways.

W. D.: Right, but what determines these different reactions?

Karen: I don't know.

W. D.: Well, psychologists have done a lot of research that tends to confirm what the ancient philosopher Epictetus said—that people are disturbed not by things but by their views of things. So your views or beliefs about your friends looking down on you determine how you feel. Does that make sense?

Karen: Yes, it does.

W. D.: So, if you want to change your feelings from shame to sorrow, what do you need to consider?

Karen: My beliefs about my friends looking down on me.

W. D.: Right, to change your feelings, you need to change your beliefs. I want first to help you to distinguish between two types of belief. One will lead to shame and other self-defeating emotions, whereas the other will lead to sorrow and other constructive emotions. Now, in order to do this, I want to digress for a moment and take you through an example in which I will distinguish between these two types of belief. Is that OK?

Karen: Fine.

W. D.: Now, I want you to imagine that you have 10 dollars in your purse and that your belief is that you prefer to have a minimum of 11 dollars at all times, but that it's not absolutely necessary for you to have 11 dollars. How will you feel about having 10 dollars when you want to have 11 dollars?

Karen: Disappointed.

W. D.:   Right, or concerned, but you wouldn't want to kill yourself, right?

Karen: Right.

W. D.:   Now, this time imagine that you believe you absolutely *must* have a minimum of 11 dollars at all times, you must, you must, you must, and you look in your purse and find that you only have 10 dollars. Now how will you feel?

Karen: Depressed.

W. D.:   Or anxious. Remember that it's the same situation but a different belief. Now imagine that you still have that same absolute belief that you must have a minimum of 11 dollars at all times, and this time you find that you have 12 dollars in your purse. Now how will you feel?

Karen: Relieved.

W. D.:   Right, or pleased. But, by holding that same belief that you absolutely must have a minimum of 11 dollars at all times, you think something that leads you to become anxious again. What do you think that thought would be?

Karen: That I might lose 2 dollars?

W. D.:   Right, or you spend 2 dollars or get robbed. Now the point of this example is that all humans, male or female, rich or poor, black or white, now and in the future, will make themselves emotionally disturbed when they don't get what they believe they *must* get. And they will also make themselves miserable when they do get it, because of their musts—because even when they have what they think they must have, they could always lose it. But when humans have nondogmatic desires and don't escalate these desires into dogmatic musts, they will constructively adjust to situations when they don't get what they want or aren't able to take effective action to try to prevent something unpleasant happening in the future.

STEP 7   Assess Beliefs

Once I felt sure that Karen could distinguish between rational and irrational beliefs, I encouraged her to extrapolate to her own situation.

W. D.:   Now keep in mind this distinction between nondogmatic desires and dogmatic musts as we apply it to your own situation, OK?

Karen: Fine.

W. D.:   Now, what do you think the must is about your friends looking down on you that leads to your shame?

Karen: They must not look down on me?

W. D.:   Right, and what kind of person do you think you would be in your own mind if they did look down on you?

Karen: No good.

STEP 8   Connect Irrational Beliefs and C

After teaching the *B-C* connection and encouraging Karen to apply it to her own situation, I next attempted to solidify the relationship between Karen's irrational beliefs and her feelings at *C*.

W. D.:   So, can you see that as long as you demand that your friends must not look down on you and as long as you believe that you are no good if they do, then you will be ashamed and tend to avoid social contact with them?

Karen: Yes, I can see that.

W. D.:   So, if you wish to change your feelings of shame to those of sorrow, what do you need to change first?

Karen: My beliefs.

W. D.:   And, more specifically, your beliefs that your friends must not look down on you and that you would be no good if they did.

STEP 9   Dispute Irrational Beliefs

The next step involved the use of the Socratic, or questioning, and didactic styles of disputing.

W. D.:   Right, now let's take these beliefs one at a time, although they're really linked. I'm going to help you to reconsider these beliefs. Let's take the first one, that your friends must not look down on you. There are basically three ways of challenging this belief. The first is to ask whether or not it is logical. Now, don't forget you have a desire, which is that you don't want your friends to look down on you, right?

Karen: Right.

W. D.:   But does it follow logically that because you don't want your friends to look down on you that they must not do so?

Karen: No, I guess not.

W. D.:   Why not?

Karen: Well, because wanting something not to happen doesn't mean it mustn't happen.

W. D.:   That's it. To demand that something mustn't happen just because we don't want it to happen is to believe in magic.

Karen: Which doesn't exist.

W. D.:   Right. Now let's consider the second way of challenging this belief, which is to ask whether or not it is consistent with reality. Now, if there really were a law of the universe that decreed that your friends absolutely would not look down on you, what could never happen?

Karen: They could never look down on me. Oh, I see . . . I'm demanding that something must not happen which could of course happen.

W. D.:   Right, that's a good insight. You would of course prefer it not to happen, but that doesn't mean that it must not happen because it always could. Now let's consider the third way of challenging this belief, which is to consider its usefulness. Now, as long as you believe that your friends must not look down on you, what consequences of holding this belief are likely?

Karen: Well, from what we discussed earlier, I'm going to be anxious about it happening and ashamed if it does happen.

W. D.:   And don't forget that it will also lead you to avoid social contact with your friends.

Karen: As has been happening.

W. D.:   Right. So the belief is going to get you into trouble. Now, to sum up: The three ways of challenging a must involve asking "Is it logical?" "Is it consistent with reality?" and "Will it give me good results?" Now we've seen that the answer to these three questions is no. But don't take my word for it—consider it for yourself. It is also important to apply these three questions to your nonabsolute preferences. First is your belief "I don't want my friends to look down on me, but

there's no reason why they must not do
so."

Karen: Well, it's logical as long as I have such a
desire.

W. D.:   Right. Now, is it consistent with reality?

Karen: Well, it is reality that I have such a desire,
so my desire exists, so, yes, it is
consistent with reality.

W. D.:   Right, and don't forget that such a belief
allows for the possibility that your friends
may look down on you, which your
dogmatic must did not allow for. Finally,
what are the likely emotional and
behavioral consequences of your belief "I
don't want my friends to look down on
me, but there's no reason why they must
not do so?"

Karen: Well, as we said earlier, it would help me
to feel sorry and would encourage me to
try to get my friends to change their
minds about me.

W. D.:   Right. Now let's use our three questions
with your second self-defeating belief: "I'm
no good if my friends look down on me."
First, is it logical to conclude that your
whole self is no good just because your
friends think badly of you?

Karen: I'm not sure I understand.

W. D.:   Well, let's assume that several of my
colleagues are listening to our session
today. Let's also assume that they not only
think badly of my therapy skills but look
down on me as a person. Do I have to
agree with them and define myself as "no
good?"

Karen: Oh, I see what you mean. I'm agreeing
with my friends' definition of me.

W. D.:   Right. Now, if your friends really do look
          down on you—and remember, we're
          assuming that they really do—they would
          have to take a part of you and consider
          that bad, then they would jump to the
          conclusion that because you had this bad
          part that all of you was bad. Is that good
          logic on their part?

Karen: No, it's not, because a part can never
          define the whole.

W. D.:   Right, and don't forget that you then
          agree with their bad logic.

Karen: Exactly.

W. D.:   You said just now that a part can never
          define the whole. That's a very good
          reason not to rate yourself at all because
          yourself is too complex to be given a
          single rating.

Karen: So it's OK to rate parts of yourself but not
          the whole?

W. D.:   Right.

Karen: So, when I say "I'm no good," I'm rating
          my whole self?

W. D.:   Right, and the alternative is to accept
          yourself as an unratable, fallible human
          being with good and bad aspects. So, if
          your friends really do look down on you,
          how can you respond in your own mind?

Karen: Let's see . . . I can accept myself as an
          unratable, fallible human being, even if
          others disapprove of me.

W. D.:   Right, and how would you feel if you
          believed that?

Karen: Sad but not ashamed.

W. D.:   Right. Now let's move on to the second
          question. If the belief "I'm no good" were

consistent with reality, what would you only be able to do in life?

Karen: No good things, and that's obviously not true.

W. D.: Right. So what's the alternative?

Karen: Again, that I'm an unratable, fallible human being who is receiving disapproval, which is bad.

W. D.: But *you're* not bad just because *it* is. Now the third question. As long as you believe that you are no good when your friends look down on you, where will that belief get you?

Karen: Anxious and ashamed.

W. D.: And again, avoiding social contact. But let's also use the three questions with the alternative beliefs. Is it logical to conclude that if your friends disapprove of you, you are still an unratable, fallible human being?

Karen: Yes, it is. Their view of me doesn't change me unless I let it. I can see that now.

W. D.: Good. Now, is the belief that you are an unratable, fallible human being in the face of their disapproval consistent with reality?

Karen: Yes, it is. As I said before, I'm still the same with or without their approval, although their approval would be nice.

W. D.: Right. Now, finally, the third point. If you believe that you are fallible and unratable in the face of your friends' disapproval, what emotional and behavioral consequences will result?

Karen: Again, I'd be sorry but not ashamed, and I'd try to reason with them rather than avoid them.

STEP 10 Prepare Your Client to Deepen Conviction in Rational Beliefs

In order to help Karen achieve more than an intellectual understanding of her problem, it was necessary to make the point that changing beliefs is a difficult process, requiring much practice.

W. D.: Now, how often do you consider you will have to challenge your self-defeating beliefs before you begin to believe in their alternatives?

Karen: Quite often.

W. D.: Right, and do you know why?

Karen: Because that's what you have to do to change a habit.

W. D.: Right. Imagine that when you were young you wanted to learn to play tennis, and your next door neighbor said that she would teach you. Unfortunately, she taught you all wrong, and, as you were keen, you continually practiced the incorrect strokes, not knowing of course that they were wrong. Years later, you found that your game was getting worse rather than better, so you decided to go to a tennis pro. She was able to diagnose the problem and showed you how to perform the strokes correctly. Now, what would you have to do to improve your tennis?

Karen: Practice the new strokes.

W. D.: Right, but would you be comfortable performing the new strokes at first?

Karen: I guess not.

W. D.: Why not?

Karen: Because I'd be used to performing the strokes incorrectly.

W. D.:   Right, they would feel natural. But would that natural feeling stop you from correcting a stroke when you realized that it was incorrect?

Karen: No.

W. D.:   Right, and it's the same with changing your beliefs. The next time you think about seeing your friends and feel like avoiding them, look for your belief "My friends must not look down on me, and I'd be no good if they did." Realize that this belief has become quite natural to you but that if you don't go along with that natural feeling, you can identify, challenge, and change that belief. You can keep doing so until the new belief "I don't want my friends to look down on me, but if they do I can still accept myself as an unratable, fallible human being" becomes more natural to you. Also, the more you act according to this new belief, the more you will gain conviction in the belief.

Karen: So I not only need to challenge the old belief in my head, I need to act on the new belief as well.

W. D.:   Exactly—until you move from believing the rational belief in your head to really feeling it in your gut and until you can act spontaneously on it.

STEP 11   Encourage Your Client to Put New Learning into Practice

Karen's ability to challenge her irrational beliefs and her understanding that it would be necessary to practice her alternative rational beliefs showed that she was ready to undertake specific homework assignments.

W. D.:   Now that takes a lot of work, so it's important for you to put into practice between sessions what you learn in sessions. Can you see the sense of that?

Karen: That's what I expected.

W. D.:   Good. Now, does it make sense to apply the three questions "Is it logical?" "Is it consistent with reality?" and "What results will it bring me?" to your self-defeating belief: "My friends must not look down on me, and I'm no good if they do?" And then to apply these three questions to your more constructive alternative: "I don't want my friends to look down on me, but there's no reason why they must not. If they do, I can still accept myself as an unratable, fallible human being."

Karen: Yes, I'd like to review those points.

W. D.:   How often would you like to do it?

Karen: How about three times a day?

W. D.:   When and where will you do it?

Karen: Just before breakfast, lunch, and dinner—wherever I happen to be eating.

W. D.:   Fine. Now, can you see any obstacles to doing this?

Karen: No. I'm sure I can do that.

W. D.:   Good. Here is a written list of the questions to use on these occasions.

STEP 12 Check Homework Assignments

At the next session, Karen revealed that she had been able to review the three questions as assigned and that she found the results helpful.

W. D.:   How did you get on with the homework assignment?

Karen: Very well. I used the three questions and can see more clearly now why the musts are self-defeating and the preferences more healthy. Also, the self-acceptance idea makes a lot of sense to me, and I've been using this idea with some of my other problems.

STEP 13   Facilitate the Working-through Process

Karen was soon ready to use behavioral assignments to overcome her feelings of shame about "being dumped." She very quickly sought out her friends and told them about the breakup of her relationship with her fiance, having practiced rational-emotive imagery first. Here she vividly imagined her friends looking down on her and began to feel ashamed, then changed this feeling to sorrow while still keeping in mind her friends' negative view of her. The imagery helped her practice changing her irrational belief to its more rational alternative. When she actually told her friends about the breakup, she was delighted to discover that they were in fact very supportive.

Karen also worked through her shame in other situations, such as work. She had previously been reluctant to ask for help whenever she could not solve a work problem. However, as she became able to dispel her shame-creating idea "My supervisor must not think badly of me, and I'd be inferior if he does," she became more willing to disclose her ignorance and to ask for help. Once again, Karen was glad to learn that her supervisor was actually pleased with her new attitude of "openness," as he called it.

Karen did not have a problem with low frustration tolerance and thus reported little difficulty in carrying out her homework assignments. Most of your clients will have more difficulty than Karen in putting into practice what they learn in therapy. We suggest that you consult Ellis (1985b) for a lengthy discussion of how to overcome client (and therapist) resistance.

EPILOGUE

We have now come to the end of our discussion. If you wish to develop your skills as a rational-emotive therapist, use RET with your clients, obtain expert supervision of your work, attend advanced RET training practica, and consult frequently the more advanced texts mentioned throughout this primer. We hope that you have found this basic introduction to RET instructive and wish you well in your future career as a rational-emotive therapist. Good luck!

Appendix

SPECIAL FEATURES OF RATIONAL-EMOTIVE THERAPY

Albert Ellis

Rational-emotive therapy (RET) has several special features that distinguish it from the cognitive therapies of Aaron Beck, Maxie Maultsby, Donald Meichenbaum, George Kelly, and other proponents of cognitive-behavior therapy, as well as from other forms of psychotherapy. Some of the special features of RET that are to be noted by RET practitioners, especially when qualifying for one of the training certificates in RET, can be observed in the areas discussed in the following pages.

SOURCES OF PSYCHOLOGICAL DISTURBANCE

RET holds that what we usually call *emotional disturbance* has important cognitive, emotive, and behavioral sources and does not purely arise from, although it is heavily influenced by, thinking. It holds that "pure" thought, "pure" emotion, and "pure" behavior virtually never exist, but are usually interactional, each including important elements of the other two. RET notably stresses *cognitive mediation*, or irrational beliefs that usually follow activating events (A's) in people's environments and that lead to emotional consequences (C's) or feelings of disturbance. But it also contends that people bring their goals, desires, and beliefs (B's) to A and that they often make new A's out of their feelings (as when they make themselves anxious about their anxiety). Similarly, their beliefs (B's) are differentially held under certain activating conditions (A's), and their emotional and behavioral consequences (C's) have to take place in some kind of environment (A's) and along with certain kinds of beliefs (B's). RET, then, sees virtually all thoughts, feelings, and behaviors as interactional, not monolithic; it also sees the A's, B's, and C's of RET—people's environments, their philosophies, and their feelings and actions—as interactional and interrelated, and practically never as thoroughly independent of one another.

RET holds that people's proneness to disturb themselves, or to react self-defeatingly to external events and internal thoughts and feelings, is both innate and acquired. People are biologically prone to think and act against their own and their society's interests, but they also partially learn to do so as a result of their social upbringing. They can easily invent irrational beliefs on their own, but they also pick them up from their parents and culture. Most of the time, they probably exacerbate their natural biological tendencies to think crookedly and behave self-sabotagingly by (often unduly) heeding environmental influences. However, people are also born with tendencies to actualize themselves: to change, to use their reasoning powers, and to push themselves to overcome environmental and self-created difficulties. Once again, they learn such self-actualizing behaviors from their parents and teachers.

Perhaps more than other forms of psychotherapy, RET emphasizes the innate tendency of people to think crookedly and engage in self-destruction and holds that this biological tendency is one of the main reasons that people frequently resist change even when they presumably want to effect it. But RET also emphasizes the innate tendency of humans to be able to choose their disturbed thoughts, feelings, and actions—and to be able to choose to change them.

In addition, RET stresses the tendency of almost all humans to create secondary as well as primary symptoms of emotional disturbance. Thus, when people make themselves seriously anxious, they frequently repeat their irrational beliefs about their anxiety and make themselves anxious about that. When they are depressed, they frequently depress themselves about their depression. Although their primary disturbances often have profound emotional, behavioral, and cognitive sources, their secondary disturbances are perhaps even more cognitive because clients *observe* their primary disturbed feelings, *think* negatively about them, and *conclude* awfulizingly about their presence and continuance.

ASSESSMENT OF DISTURBANCES

RET tends to employ at times all the assessment procedures used by other cognitive-behavior therapies, but it can also be done with a minimum of these procedures in some instances. This is largely because RET favors RET itself as an important means of assessment and holds that, in many (but not all) cases, zeroing in on some of the client's irrational beliefs can be highly diagnostic and can particularly indicate how and under what conditions the client is likely to react to psychotherapy. For example, clients who have great difficulty in acknowledging their irrational beliefs, in recognizing that such beliefs contribute significantly to their disturbances, and in forcefully and persistently disputing them (as they are shown to do in RET) will usually be different from other clients. Their problems in reacting to RET will produce salient diagnostic and prognostic information.

RET notably distinguishes between appropriate and inappropriate feelings when people react to some unfortunate set of events and tends to define feelings such as sorrow, regret, frustration, and annoyance as appropriate and feelings such as anxiety, depression, hostility, self-downing, and self-pity as inappropriate. RET practitioners therefore actively look for appropriate and inappropriate feelings and may at times show clients that it is appropriate to be mournful or concerned rather than depressed or horrified—and therefore, in RET terms, they really do not have a serious emotional problem. Conversely, an RET practitioner may refuse to try to help clients become unconcerned about, say, holding a job or the state of their physical health because lack of concern may be considered inappropriate and harmful rather than appropriate and healthy.

LOOKING FOR IRRATIONAL BELIEFS

Although virtually all systems of cognitive or cognitive-behavior therapy help clients look for irrational beliefs, self-defeating ideas, or dysfunctional cognitions, RET takes a somewhat unique stand in this respect:

1. RET holds that almost all kinds of irrationalities —including unrealistic or antiempirical and illogical conclusions—tend to produce poor results for individuals and social groups. Thus, people who come to psychotherapy and who are seen as being "emotionally disturbed" do not merely have *some* irrational beliefs but also almost invariably have *certain kinds* of highly prevalent irrationalities. According to RET, the main kinds of irrational beliefs that lead to disturbance are absolutistic and unconditional shoulds, oughts, musts, demands, commands, and expectations. More specifically, almost all people who are diagnosed as neurotic (and as moderately borderline personalities) absolutistically and dogmatically command that they themselves *must* do well and be approved by significant others, that others *have to* treat them considerately and fairly, and that conditions of living have *got to* be reasonably easy and enjoyable.

2. If, RET hypothesizes, people stayed rigorously with preferences, wishes, and desires, including strong ones, and did not resort to absolutistic shoulds and musts, they would rarely, if ever, become neurotic. RET therefore invariably looks for, and helps clients look for, their evaluative irrational ideas, not merely their nonevaluative overgeneralities and unrealistic notions. Thus, it is highly irrational to say, descriptively and nonevaluatively, "The earth is flat," and one will probably get into some kind of difficulty if one holds this idea. But one will not tend to be emotionally disturbed unless one adds something like "The earth is

flat—as it *must* be" or "I *can't stand* the earth's being round—and therefore it isn't." RET does not contend that people cannot be disturbed without their subscribing to absolutistic evaluations instead of staying with their relativistic preferences, but it looks for and virtually always finds such unconditional evaluations when people are seriously anxious, depressed, hating, or self-downing.

3. Feelings of emotional disturbance also result from irrational beliefs other than absolutistic evaluations (i.e., from awfulizing, I-can't-stand-it-itis, and damnation of oneself and others). But these kinds of irrational beliefs seem, in just about every case, to be derivatives of explicit or implicit absolutistic musts and would rarely, if ever, exist without them. Thus, when I irrationally hold that "The earth must be flat!" I then tend to conclude logically, if erroneously, that (a) "It is *awful* if the earth is not as flat as it must be!" (b) "I *can't stand it* when the earth is not as flat as it has to be!" and (c) "I'm *no good* if I don't see the earth as being as flat as it must be!"

4. In addition to absolutistic or "musturbatory" thinking, people often contribute to their disturbances with antiempirical or unrealistic inferences. For example, they tell themselves, "Because I failed a few times, I will always fail." They personalize, overgeneralize, resort to non sequiturs, and use always-and-never thinking about their strong desires. But they especially do so when they escalate their desires into absolutistic demands and musts. Irrational, unrealistic, and illogical inference is itself an important aspect of human behavior and results in many poor outcomes. But unless it is tied to absolutistic musts and commands and to human evaluations, it does not usually result in what we call emotional disturbance.

DISPUTING IRRATIONAL BELIEFS

RET emphasizes the use of scientific method and of logico-empirical disputing to help people change the irrational beliefs that lead them to disturbance. It often actively questions and challenges all kinds and levels of irrational beliefs, but it particularly challenges musts and necessities and helps people change them into desires and preferences. It favors science and the scientific method in several ways that other kinds of therapy do not favor or mention:

1. It holds that people who consistently employ scientific, flexible, nondogmatic, nonabsolutistic thinking about themselves and others are only minimally disturbed and that dogma, inflexibility, and refusal to accept reality are the essence of much serious disturbance.

2. It teaches the scientific method of questioning and disputing irrational hypotheses to as many of its clients as will accept and use this method and shows them how to apply it when the therapist is not present.

3. It accepts the mildly and moderately religious beliefs and values of its clients and shows them how to live undisturbedly (if inelegantly) with religious, mystical, or superstitious ideas. But it unmasks devout religiosity—whether theological, political, economic, or social—and shows people how to combat dogma and absolutism.

4. In some special cases, it may reluctantly use nonscientific and religious views that are antiempirical but that may help people ameliorate their disturbance and do them more good than harm.

THERAPEUTIC RELATIONSHIP

RET favors the building of a good rapport with clients, uses empathic listening and reflection of feeling, and particularly uses strong encouragement to help clients look at themselves and change. At the same time, it acknowledges the dangers of building too warm or close a relationship between client and therapist. (Many clients tend to have a dire need for everyone's, including the therapist's, approval; therefore, the therapist's showing favoritism may help accentuate this need.)

RET acknowledges that the therapist also may have a dire need for clients' approval and may consequently hold back from doing active disputing of the clients' irrational beliefs and from giving them onerous homework assignments. RET therefore encourages therapists to look at their own motives for building overly warm relationships with clients. At the same time, RET especially holds that the therapist had better have unconditional positive regard or acceptance for all clients—no matter how obnoxiously they may behave in or out of therapy. It allows therapists to evaluate clients' acts and thoughts, but not to rate them globally as humans, nor especially to denigrate their selves, beings, or essences in any way.

RET often tries to show clients that they are equal and active collaborators with the therapist in looking at and changing themselves. At the same time, it sees the therapist as a highly active-directive teacher, who knows more about human personality and its disturbances than the clients and who therefore had often better take the lead in explaining, interpreting, and disputing, as well as in urging the clients to come up with better solutions to their problems.

MULTIMODAL AND COMPREHENSIVE USE OF TECHNIQUES

RET has a distinct theory of human disturbance and of how it may most efficiently be reduced. But its theory, as discussed earlier, is interactive and multimodal, and sees emotions, thoughts, and behaviors as transacting and including one another. Hence RET has always been multimodal in its uses of many therapeutic techniques: cognitive, emotive, and behavioral. Because it emphasizes the biological as well as social sources of human disturbance, it frequently favors the use of medication and of physical (as well as mental) techniques of psychotherapy, including diet, exercise, and relaxation techniques.

At the same time, RET is highly selective in the methods it employs and only occasionally uses a method because it works (e.g., positive thinking). Instead, RET looks at the long-range as well as the short-range effects of employing various methods, considers many techniques as more palliative than curative (e.g., cognitive distraction), and tries to emphasize those methods that lead to a profound philosophical and emotional change and that help clients *get* better in addition to *feel* better. It starts most clients off with those RET methods that usually work best with certain people most of the time; if these fail, it goes on to the use of different methods. It doesn't compulsively choose one or several methods with virtually all clients all of the time, and it fully realizes that some clients, such as those with psychoses or mental retardation, may not be able to use some of the better methods and may have to settle for more palliative techniques.

Almost all forms of psychotherapy try particularly to help clients with ego problems—that is, those clients with feelings of anxiety, depression, and self-downing. RET, although specializing in such problems, also looks for difficulties associated with low frustration tolerance (or what RET calls *discomfort anxiety*). It assumes that most clients have both ego anxiety and discomfort anxiety, and when one is prominent it looks for (but does not necessarily always find) the other. It uses some of its methods to combat ego and some to combat discomfort disturbance, and it looks for the interrelationship between these two somewhat distinct, but overlapping, kinds of problems. Thus, RET shows clients how to accept themselves when they are doing poorly, but it also shows them how to give up their low frustration tolerance about working therapeutically to change themselves so that the latter problem does not interfere with self-acceptance.

EMOTIVE ASPECTS

In keeping with its comprehensive and multimodal character, RET almost invariably uses a number of emotive as well as cognitive and behavioral techniques. This is because its theory emphasizes not only repetition but force in self-statements and holds that when people feel highly emotional, and particularly emotionally disturbed, and when they hang onto their disturbances, they forcefully, vigorously, and vividly tell themselves or implicitly believe musturbatory statements. Therefore, they had better use many strong, dramatic, evocative methods of changing themselves, and RET specializes in seeing that they do so. It usually sees that clients *forcefully* dispute their irrational beliefs and that they *actively* get in touch with and work on changing their feelings. RET practitioners, moreover, often *powerfully* show clients how they are disturbing themselves and how they will continue to be disturbed unless they vigorously strive to modify themselves.

Toward this end, RET usually favors a number of emotive methods, including rational-emotive imagery, shame-attacking exercises, role playing, strong self-statements, therapeutic encouragement, group support, and various other affective techniques. But, as previously mentioned, it employs these methods not only for their immediate benefits but also to help clients make a profound affective-philosophical change that will presumably be of a lasting nature. At the same time, RET tends to take a dim view of several popular emotive methods, such as the instigation and expression of hostile feelings, because it holds that these methods are likely to do more harm than good.

HUMANISTIC ASPECTS

Unlike some of the other cognitive-behavior therapies, RET takes a definite humanistic-existential approach. It is not purely objective, scientific, or technique-centered in that it adheres to the following principles:

1. It deals with disturbed *human* evaluations, emotions, and behaviors. It sees humans as the basic creators or inventors of their own emotional problems and therefore as *humanly* capable of minimizing these problems.

2. It is highly rational and scientific but uses rationality and science in the service of humans in an attempt to enable them to live and be happy. It is hedonistic but espouses long-range instead of short-range hedonism so that people may achieve the pleasure of the moment and the future, and arrive at maximum freedom and discipline.

3. It hypothesizes that nothing superhuman probably exists and that devout belief in superhuman agencies tends to foster dependency and increase emotional disturbance.

4. It assumes that no humans, whatever their antisocial or obnoxious behavior, are damnable or subhuman. It respects and accepts all people just because they are alive and human.

5. It attempts to help people maximize their individuality, freedom, self-interest, and self-control rather than to submit to the control and direction of others (including their therapists). At the same time, it tries to help people live in an involved, committed, and selectively loving manner with other humans and to foster social as well as individual interest.

6. It particularly emphasizes the importance of will and choice in human affairs, even though it accepts the likelihood that some human behavior is partially determined by biological, social, and other forces.

VIEW OF SELF-ACCEPTANCE

Whereas most other psychotherapies attempt to help people achieve self-esteem, RET is skeptical of this concept and tries instead to help them achieve what it calls *self-acceptance*—or, better, to refuse to rate their selves, their beings, or their essences at all but only to rate their acts, deeds, and performances:

1. Because most people automatically and unconsciously rate themselves as well as their acts and often feel that they must continue to do this, RET teaches these individuals that their self-rating had better depend solely on their aliveness and humanity. That is, people can rate themselves as "good," if they insist on rating themselves at all, just because they are alive and human.

2. RET shows people that no matter what criteria they rate themselves upon—whether it be external (e.g., success or accomplishment), internal (e.g., character or emotional stability), or supernatural (e.g., acceptance by Jesus or God)—they really *choose* these criteria. Therefore, they can more elegantly accept themselves merely because they choose to do so and require no other criteria whatever.

3. As noted, RET encourages people to refuse to rate their
selves, totality, beings, or essences at all but to rate
only their acts, deeds, and performances. By elim-
inating all kinds of self-ratings and merely rating
acts as "good" when they are self-helping and "bad"
when they are self-defeating, people can most elegantly
solve the problem of rating—or not rating—themselves.

4. Strong refusal to rate oneself or one's being at all can
be achieved by people's merely holding the following
beliefs: (a) "I am alive"; (b) "I would like to continue to
remain alive"; (c) "I would prefer to be happily instead
of unhappily alive"; (d) "I can do a number of things
that will help me survive happily and a number of
things that will not help me, so I shall label the first set
as 'good' and the second set as 'bad' or 'unfortunate'";
and (e) "Beyond this, I don't have to go; I shall thereby
try to accept myself and enjoy myself—but not try to
prove myself."

VIEW OF EFFICIENCY AND ELEGANCE
IN PSYCHOTHERAPY

RET, unlike some other types of psychotherapy, especially strives for efficiency and elegance in therapy. To this
end, it holds the following:

1. RET aims not merely for symptom removal but also for
a profound change in the basic philosophy that largely
creates people's symptoms—and that usually also
contributes to some other less highlighted symptoms.

2. RET tries to alleviate or remove most disturbances
permanently, not transiently, though it acknowledges
that people have a tendency, from time to time, to
retrogress and reinstitute their symptoms once they
have originally minimized or eliminated them.

3. RET tries to help as many of its clients as feasible make
profound philosophical changes that will deter them
from creating new disturbances in the future.

4. RET shows clients how they can quickly see what they
do to create new symptoms or recreate old ones and

how they can promptly alleviate these disturbances. It motivates people to remove their symptoms as quickly as is feasible and to block their reoccurrence. Once such symptoms do reoccur, RET encourages clients to get to work promptly to understand how they recreated them and to work at alleviating them.

5. RET tries to develop methods of elegant psychotherapy that require relatively little therapeutic time and effort and that produce maximum results quickly and efficiently.

6. RET tries to develop and promote psychoeducational methods that can help clients help themselves and that also can be applied to large numbers of people rather than only to individual clients. It specializes in bibliotherapy, audiotherapy, videotherapy, talks, workshops, courses, and other media presentations in which some of the main RET teachings can be effectively used with large groups of disturbed or disturbable individuals.

BEHAVIORAL METHODS

RET almost always uses behavioral techniques of therapy, but it particularly favors in vivo forms of desensitization rather than purely imaginative forms of systematic desensitization, especially with difficult clients who resist other methods. More specifically:

1. It holds that people will rarely change their disturbance-creating philosophies unless they strongly and steadily *act* against them.

2. It frequently urges clients to make themselves deliberately uncomfortable (e.g., in performing exercise or sports) until they finally become comfortable and, perhaps, enjoying.

3. It often encourages people to act against their disturbances implosively (i.e., flooding) rather than gradually because that kind of quickly repeated action will sometimes prove to be most helpful.

RET uses behavioral reinforcement procedures in many instances but often uses them differently than do other schools of cognitive-behavior therapy:

1. It is wary of using love or approval as a reinforcer because many people may thereby become more suggestible and less autonomous and scientific.

2. It tries to help people think through for themselves and decide on their own goals and purposes—and hence to become less suggestible and less reinforceable by external influences.

3. It endeavors to help people do things (e.g., art and science) for the intrinsic enjoyment of doing them more than for the extrinsic rewards of, say, money or fame.

4. It encourages clients who are not easily reinforceable to use, instead of or in addition to rewards, stiff penalties when they want to change dysfunctional behaviors. But it tries to make very clear that penalties are not to be used as punishments and do not include any ideas of undeservingness or damnation.

MULTIPLICITY OF COGNITIVE METHODS

Although RET favors disputing, skepticism, and the use of logical-empirical methods of science in helping people to see and to surrender their basic irrational beliefs, it also employs many other cognitive methods of therapy also designed to help people change their self-defeating thinking, emoting, and behaving:

1. It often uses positive self-statements or rational beliefs and helps clients to write these down, think about them, and steadily and strongly repeat them to themselves. For example, if a client irrationally believed, "I must be loved by so-and-so in order to accept myself," an RET practitioner would (a) illustrate how to actively dispute this idea; (b) ask, "What alternate rational statements could you make to yourself instead of this irrational statement?"; and (c) have the client write down a list of rational coping

statements (e.g., "I do not need what I want" or "It is highly desirable to be loved by so-and-so, but I can also live happily without that love") and keep going over these statements every day until the client actually tended to believe them.

2. It uses many forms of cognitive distraction (e.g., relaxation methods, yoga, meditation, reading, creative writing, socializing, etc.) to help clients temporarily give up their obsessions with self-defeating ideas.

3. It often uses a good deal of philosophical discussion, including existential dialogues, with clients.

4. It teaches people how to do problem solving—including how to go back to A's and change them for the better.

5. It uses semantic approaches to show people how to stop using overgeneralized language such as "I *always* fail" or "Good things *never* happen to me."

6. It uses imaging techniques, including positive imagery (in which people are able to imagine themselves succeeding rather than failing at an important task) and negative imagery (as in rational-emotive imagery, in which clients imagine some of the worst things that could happen to them and make themselves appropriately sorry and regretful instead of inappropriately panicked).

7. It employs modeling methods, through which clients are shown how to help themselves and how to do RET by observing others successfully do so.

In employing these cognitive methods, as well as in its emotive and behavioral techniques, RET practitioners are rarely satisfied with symptom improvement, even when this is radical and startling. Their main goal with most clients most of the time is to try to help these individuals achieve a profound attitudinal or philosophical change—to internalize a new way of looking at themselves, at others, and at the world so that they seldom seriously disturb themselves about anything that may happen to them and so that, when they do, they immediately acknowledge their own contribution to this disturbance and get themselves to work at undisturbing themselves. Therefore, RET is not only a theory and practice of psychotherapy but a philosophy that holds that human disturbance is largely, although not completely, self-created and that most people are capable of uncreating their own disturbances and of stubbornly refusing to upset themselves severely about almost anything for the rest of their lives. RET acknowledges that most clients will only partially accept and internalize this elegant attitude, but it strives to help as many as possible to do so.

REFERENCES AND RECOMMENDED READING

Bard, J. A. (1980). *Rational-emotive therapy in practice.* Champaign, IL: Research Press.

Beck, A. T. (1976). *Cognitive therapy and the emotional disorders.* New York: International Universities Press.

†Bernard, M. E., & Joyce, M. R. (1984). *Rational-emotive therapy with children and adolescents.* New York: Wiley-Interscience.

Crawford, T., & Ellis, A. (1989). A dictionary of rational-emotive feelings and behaviors. *Journal of Rational-Emotive and Cognitive Behavior Therapy, 7,* 3–27.

Dryden, W. (1986). Language and meaning in RET. *Journal of Rational-Emotive Therapy, 4,* 131–142.

*Dryden, W. (1987). *Counselling individuals: The rational-emotive approach.* London: Taylor & Francis.

---

*Resources recommended for use with general populations.
†Resources recommended for use with specific client populations.

Ellis, A. (1976). The biological basis of human irrationality. *Journal of Individual Psychology, 32,* 145–168.

Ellis, A. (1984a). The essence of RET—1984. *Journal of Rational-Emotive Therapy, 2*(1), 19–25.

Ellis, A. (1984b). *How to maintain and enhance your rational-emotive therapy gains.* New York: Institute for Rational-Emotive Therapy.

Ellis, A. (1985a). Expanding the ABC's of rational-emotive therapy. In M. J. Mahoney & A. Freeman (Eds.), *Cognition and psychotherapy* (pp. 313–323). New York: Plenum.

Ellis, A. (1985b). *Overcoming resistance: Rational-emotive therapy with difficult clients.* New York: Springer.

*Ellis, A. (1988). *How to stubbornly refuse to make yourself miserable about anything—Yes, anything.* Secaucus, NJ: Lyle Stuart.

*Ellis, A., & Dryden, W. (1987). *The practice of rational-emotive therapy.* New York: Springer.

*Ellis, A., & Grieger, R. (Eds.). (1977). *Handbook of rational-emotive therapy* (Vol. 1). New York: Springer.

*Ellis, A., & Grieger, R. (Eds.). (1986). *Handbook of rational-emotive therapy* (Vol. 2). New York: Springer.

†Ellis, A., McInerney, J. F., DiGiuseppe, R., & Yeager, R. J. (1988). *Rational-emotive therapy with alcoholics and substance abusers.* New York: Pergamon.

†Ellis, A., Sichel, J., Yeager, R. J., Dimattia, D., & DiGiuseppe, R. (1989). *Rational-emotive couples therapy.* New York: Pergamon.

Gendlin, E. T. (1978). *Focusing.* New York: Everest.

*Grieger, R. M., & Boyd, J. (1980). *Rational-emotive therapy: A skills-based approach.* New York: Van Nostrand Reinhold.

*Hauck, P. A. (1980). *Brief counseling with RET.* Philadelphia: Westminster.

†Huber, C. H., & Baruth, L. G. (1989). *Rational-emotive family therapy: A systems perspective.* New York: Springer.

Maultsby, M. C., Jr., & Ellis, A. (1974). *Techniques for using rational-emotive imagery.* New York: Institute for Rational-Emotive Therapy.

Passons, W. R. (1975). *Gestalt approaches in counseling.* New York: Holt, Rinehart & Winston.

Trexler, L. D. (1976). Frustration is a fact, not a feeling. *Rational Living, 11*(2), 19–22.

*Walen, S. R., DiGiuseppe, R., & Wessler, R. L. (1980). *A practitioner's guide to rational-emotive therapy.* New York: Oxford University Press.

*Wessler, R. A., & Wessler, R. L. (1980). *The principles and practice of rational-emotive therapy.* San Francisco: Jossey-Bass.

ABOUT THE AUTHORS

Windy Dryden, Ph.D., is a senior lecturer in the Department of Psychology, Goldsmiths' College, University of London. He is co-founder of the *Journal of Cognitive Psychotherapy: An International Quarterly* and trains therapists in RET for the Institute for Rational-Emotive Therapy in the United Kingdom. He has authored or edited 30 books and has written numerous chapters and articles for professional publications.

Raymond DiGiuseppe, Ph.D., ABPP, is an associate professor of psychology and Director of the Graduate Program in School Psychology at St. John's University in New York. He is also Director of Research and Training at the Institute for Rational-Emotive Therapy and Chair of the International Training Standards and Review Committee for Rational-Emotive Therapy. He has co-authored four books and has contributed over 20 chapters and articles to the professional literature.